THE NATURE OF SOCIOLOGY

Marcel Mauss

THE NATURE OF SOCIOLOGY

Two Essays

Translated by

William Jeffrey

Introduction by

Mike Gane

Durkheim Press/Berghahn Books
New York • Oxford

First published in 2005 by

Berghahn Books

www.berghahnbooks.com

© 2005 Durkheim Press

Library of Congress Cataloging-in-Publication Data
A catalog record for this book is available from the Library of Congress

British Library Cataloguing in Publication Data
A catalogue record for this book is available from the British Library.

Printed in the United States on acid-free paper
ISBN 1–57181–659–3 hardback

Contents

Preface and Acknowledgements

The British Centre for Durkheimian Studies in Oxford has made one of its aims the promotion of the work of Marcel Mauss. It has done this by holding conferences concerned with his work and by translating his lesser-known writings into English. In conjunction with the Durkheim Press and Berghahn Books, the Centre is pleased to see published here two of his essays, both concerned with the nature of sociology as a discipline in its own right.

As in previous books generated by the Centre, the production of the present volume is very much the result of a group effort of members. In particular, warm thanks are extended to Mike Gane, Nick Allen and Dominique Lussier, who in various ways, obvious and not so obvious, have contributed to this book.

The English translations of the two essays by Marcel Mauss, which constitute this book, were made by William Jeffrey Jr. while he was Law Librarian and Professor of Law at the University of Cincinnati. He was born in Sloan, Iowa, in 1921 and studied Law, as well as Library Science, at the University of Chicago. Before going to Cincinnati he was Law Librarian at Drake University in Des Moines, Iowa, and subsequently at Yale Law Library. He died in Cincinnati in 1983.

His major interest was in American legal history but a fascination with languages led him to translate material not available in English. Prominent were French sociological works particularly relating to law. One notable translation was of Durkheim's article of 1901, 'Two Laws of Penal Evolution', which appeared in 1969 in the *University of Cincinnati Law Review*.

Of his translations, those relating to members of the Durkheim School were deposited in the archives of the British Centre for Durkheimian Studies in Oxford in 2002 and 2003 by his widow, Mrs Margaret Jeffrey. She has given the Centre permission to publish them and the Centre very much appreciates her generosity in this matter.

The translations reproduced here have been emended in some places by Nick Allen, whose work on Marcel Mauss is well known.

Finally, the Centre is indeed grateful to the Président de *L'Année Sociologique* for permission to translate into English, Marcel Mauss, 'Divisions et proportions des divisions de la sociologie', (*L'Année sociologique*, série 2, 1927, pp. 98–176).

W.S.F. Pickering

Introduction

Mike Gane

Today there is no doubt that the reputation of Mauss (1872–1950) is significant and growing. There is a marked divergence of opinion, however, on the nature of his contribution and influence.

On the one hand stands a strong body of opinion which holds that Mauss's work did not amount to a systematic and coherent general theory and method, but was influential through the specific inspiration of unique studies, such as *The Gift* (1966, 1990). On the other hand, there is another appropriation that is divided into two lines of assessment, but both suggest there was a profound unity in Mauss's teaching and research that amounted to a systematic theory. One line of this argument is that Mauss's general theory was a contribution to structuralism (an argument presented in Lévi-Strauss's famous *Introduction to the Work of Marcel Mauss* (1987)). The other line is that which suggests that the inner core of Mauss's theory was identified by Bataille, Caillois and others at the end of the 1930s in the famous Collège de Sociologie, and subsequently elaborated by general theorists of symbolic exchange such as Baudrillard. Writers from both lines – Lévi-Strauss to Godelier and Bataille to Baudrillard – have taken Mauss's anthropological theory and wedded it to a version of Marxist theory, a step that Mauss himself would certainly not have thought legitimate. The methodological guidelines he drew up were supposed to deal with this possibility. The fact that they seemed to have failed implies that the legacy of Mauss is sometimes seen as uncertain or even paradoxical (Cazeneuve 1968). Did Mauss's contribution constitute a coherent whole, or was it made up of individual unique studies that could potentially be made the basis of further and conflicting elaborations?

A reading of his methodological writings, principally those included in this collection, is essential to understanding his thought in the widest sense. If today there is not only a renewed interest in Mauss, and one that goes beyond any one individual study such as *The Gift*, it is also an interest that in many cases seeks to relocate Mauss in the context of the sociological – not the Marxist tradition. These reassessments are possible with the publication of Mauss's collected political writings (1997) in the context of the collapse of international communism and the changed political horizons of the new millennium. The indications of this new interest are to be found in studies such as the conference collection edited by James and Allen (1998), and Allen's *Categories and Classifications: Maussian Reflections on the Social* (2000), but also in France the intellectual biography *Marcel Mauss* by Marcel Fournier (1994), Bruno Karsenti's *L'Homme Totale: Sociologie, Anthropologie et Philosophie chez Marcel Mauss* (1997) and Camille Tarot's *De Durkheim à Mauss: l'Invention de Symbolique* (1999). A translation of Mauss's important thesis, *On Prayer*, was published in 2003.

Here, in this collection, is included the essay entitled 'Sociology' by Fauconnet and Mauss which was published in 1901 (in *La Grande Encyclopédie* – for background on this publication see Tollebeek 2002:343–45), and the essay 'Sociology: Its Divisions and Their Relative Weightings', which was published in 1927. In reading these two essays we are in a position to judge to what extent there was a shift in the nature of the work of the school over a twenty-five-year period divided by the First World War.

Mauss, as is well known, has become principally associated with the discipline of anthropology, while Durkheim remains a key founder of modern sociology but neither separated the two disciplines. Mauss himself explicitly states in 1927 that the separation of anthropology from sociology would constitute a danger. But today we may ask, did Mauss in fact contribute in some ways to laying the ground for this separation, which became more pronounced after his death? And, given Mauss's own growing academic specialisation in anthropological work and theory, did he provide adequate methodological safeguards against the inappropriate generalisation of his own anthropological analyses within the wider domain of sociology?

These questions themselves remain paradoxical, since the Durkheimians made it a key feature of their project to reflect on their practices as sociologists and anthropologists, and wrote a great many texts on their methodological principles. Indeed, the rules they created were applied not only to specific procedures such as how to observe, but also to the organisation of the work of the entire project. They asked the question: what is the fundamental objective of sociology, and how should a school of sociology divide the work and arrange specialist tasks in a coherent whole? As Mauss reported in his obituary of Fauconnet (Mauss 1999), there was a project around the year 1900 for a consideration of the methods of the new school which was to be a group effort involving himself, Durkheim and Fauconnet. Of this project only individual papers were published and these were never collected together, thus the project never achieved the coherence of a new statement of orientation that was originally hoped for.

What was the intellectual situation in 1900 in the Durkheim group? In terms of publications the period around 1900 was dominated by the appearance of the *Année sociologique*. Between 1898 and 1913 twelve volumes were published, although the volumes that contained significant analyses or articles ended with volume 9 in 1906. A conspectus of the contributions of Durkheim and Mauss indicate that their work was dominated by questions of the nature of the elemental forms of social and cultural structure. The first volume of 1898 contained Durkheim's essay on the origins of the incest taboo. The second published Durkheim's essay on the definition of religious phenomena, and Mauss and Hubert's essay on sacrifice. The next major items by Durkheim appeared in volume 4 (1902), containing Durkheim's essay on penal evolution, and in volume 5 with Durkheim's essay on totemism. Volume 6 (1903) contained Durkheim and Mauss on 'Primitive Classification'. Volume 7 (1904) contained Mauss and Hubert's essay on magic. Volume 8 (1905) contained Durkheim's essay on 'The Matrimonial Organisation of Australian Societies', volume 9 (1906) contained Mauss and Beuchat's essay 'Seasonal Variations of the Eskimo'. Incontestably the essays published in the new journal were dominated by themes of religion, ritual, classification and sanctions in 'primitive' societies.

No further important articles appeared in the first series of the journal. The subsequent volumes were published in 1907 (volume 10), three years later in 1910 (volume 11) and a last volume (number 12), was published in 1913; they were henceforth completely dominated by reviews. From this conspectus we can see that the focus of published work in this period was certainly dominated by what now would be called anthropological topics and concerns. A number of commentators have noticed the shift in these years to a concern with non-European elemental forms, so that in the words of Paul Vogt, 'French sociology was done largely without extensive reference to modern French society' (in Hamilton 1990, I:178). Others have drawn parallel conclusions, pointing to the systematic absence of sociological analysis of key institutional formations of modern societies, such as political parties and power structures (Lukes, in Durkheim 1982:22). But the overall strategy of the Durkheimians is clear: it is to establish a new type of comparative and evolutionary sociology that would avoid the errors of Comte's positivist sociology on the one hand, and all the variations of individualistic methodologies on the other. Like Comte, the Durkheimians thought reflection on method essential to social science, but unlike Comte they considered method a dynamic element of the practice of sociology that had to change as the science itself developed.

In fact, around 1900 – following closely on the long and innovative methodological reflections in his study *Suicide*, published in 1897 – Durkheim himself published a number of interrelated methodological essays, including 'Sociology in France in the Nineteenth Century' (1901), 'Sociology and its

Scientific Field' (1900), and 'On the Objective Method in Sociology' (1901 – republished as the second Preface to a new edition of *The Rules of Sociological Method*). In this Preface Durkheim returned to his famous discussions of the object of sociology and the conception of the 'social fact' but only to draw attention to the new conception – sociology as the science of institutions – developed by Mauss and Fauconnet in1901: 'In fact, without doing violence to the meaning of the word, one may term an institution all the beliefs and modes of behavior instituted by the collectivity; sociology can then be defined as the science of institutions, their genesis and their functioning' (Durkheim 1982:45).

The contribution of Fauconnet and Mauss of 1901('Sociology', 1901, in *La Grande Encyclopédie*) was conceived as part of a larger statement of the school (Gane 1988:30–38). This project for a general presentation of the sociological project around 1900 is described by Mauss in his 'Intellectual self-portrait' (in Besnard 1983, and in James and Allen 1998). Initially he says there was to be a sequel to Durkheim's *Rules*, a book in three parts. The first part was the essay 'Sociology' which appeared in *La Grande Encyclopédie* (Durkheim's letters offering advice to Mauss on this article are now available in Durkheim 1998:257–64). The second part, said Mauss, 'is the article by Durkheim and Fauconnet, in fact written by the three of us, which is entitled 'History of Sociology and the Social Sciences' (1903, a translation can be found in Durkheim, 1982:175–208). 'The third part has never been published' (Mauss in Besnard 1983:150–51). In the recently published obituary notice Mauss wrote for Fauconnet in 1939, Mauss says that the third part was called 'Les divisions de la Sociologie'. The three parts were to be published together as an 'Introduction à la Sociologie' (Mauss 1999:28).

The role of rules of method for Durkheim and Mauss was to reflect on and to control the process of scientific analysis from beginning to end, without at the same time creating obstacles to the necessary free action of the scientific imagination. At each stage of the development of sociological science it was essential to stand back and to examine definitions, the rules of observation and of analysis, and of the division of labour between the branches of the activity of the school. Thus it can be seen that each attempt at methodological reflection was an attempt to guide, even inspire, the work of the school. This mode of reflection does not exactly provide résumés of specific studies, but it does provide an official manifesto of the orientations of the school. Thus for example *The Rules of Sociological Method* (1895) clearly reworked guideline materials from *The Division of Labour in Society* (1893) in preparation for the next study, *Suicide* (1897). The various methodological writings around 1900, which include the essay by Paul Fauconnet and Mauss published in this collection, evidently relate to the studies that the school was engaged in after the publication of Durkheim's *Suicide*, and include the first essays by Mauss. It is important to compare, then, the phrasing of Fauconnet and Mauss in 'Sociology' with that of earlier formulations. The objective in their essay was to present sociology as something that already had an important established reality, and yet was open to further significant development. 'Sociology' certainly follows some of Durkheim's ideas in *The Rules* very closely. Given that the project involved Mauss, Fauconnet and Durkheim himself, the texts are also ones which announce a new collective endeavour of a team of sociologists. The orientations of this new school in fact draw upon some distinctive ideas. A change of emphasis, however, is noticeable if we consider four essential ideas which were promoted by Durkheim in the mid-1890s.

The first of these principles mandate the sociologist to approach the objects of the discipline with a special frame of mind: social phenomena ('social facts') are to be considered as being external to each individual. Indeed there is a mark or sign of this externality in social facts which must be found, identified and then must guide the sociologist as a focus in the subsequent analysis. A mark, such as the obligatory character of such phenomena, indicates the real necessity of the social relationship or action involved. Evidently, according to the Durkheimians, the principal errors that sociologists hitherto have been tempted to make are those arising from assuming that analysis must follow the free actions of individuals. The strategy of the Durkheimians was to extend the causality principle into the social domain – initially by guiding analysis towards social action that is most obviously socially caused, here interpreted as that mode of action clearly independent (either negatively or positively) of individual, free volition. Durkheim's formulation of 1895 in *The Rules of Sociological Method* suggested that the object of sociology, the 'social fact', can be defined as 'any way of acting, whether fixed or not, capable of exerting over the individual an external constraint' (Durkheim 1982:59). This very striking formulation gave rise to considerable debate, some of which Durkheim thought badly misguided. In his 'Second Preface' to the *The Rules*, in 1901, which tried to play down the importance of coercion as an aspect of constraint, he said that the 'coercive power that we attribute to the social fact represents so small a part of its totality that it can equally well display the opposite characteristic. Institutions', he said, 'place contraints upon us, and yet we find satisfaction in the way they function, and in that very constraint' (ibid.:47). The Durkheimians did not abandon the principle of externality even if they introduced subtleties in relation to the notion of constraint.

A second feature was the development of a set of rules about the nature and quality of the data available to the sociologist. Having emphasised the necessity for the sociologist to study things not ideas, the sociologist must also be trained to tackle the problem of the reliability of information. In fact, in Durkheim's essays on method the question of the nature of sources and robustness of information is rarely examined. It is pushed into the background while either concerns of a more philosophical nature take precedence, or Durkheim simply indicates a preference for legal data over, for example, literary descriptions (ibid.:83). Mauss and Fauconnet on the other hand, begin the discussion of the

reliability of sources in a much more systematic way. And this is continued by
Mauss in his subsequent writings (for example the elaboration of what he calls
the 'critical method' (2003:39)).

A third major feature apparent in Durkheim's writings of the 1890s,
certainly in his methodological statements, is the theme of social pathology. A
chapter is devoted to this theme in the *The Rules*, where clearly it functions to
link analysis with action. One of the key objectives for sociology, he says, is its
potential to identify social health. This theme is not abandoned at the turn of
the century, for in his 1902 'Preface to the Second Edition' of *The Division of
Labour in Society*, he indicated, in one of his most clearly diagnostic texts, the
problems following the absence of corporative institutions in modern France,
producing 'the most far reaching consequences... [for] the general health of
the social body' (1964:29). Mauss himself was to emphasise a number of times
that this was the central practical and political recommendation of Durkheim.
But there is no place in Mauss's method for this category, and it does not figure
in the methodological writings published under his name. The entry in *La
Grande Encyclopédie*, translated here, even though it discusses all the other
categories of method established by Durkheim in *The Rules*, does not include a
consideration of the rules for the analysis of social pathology. It is important, if
we are to establish the nature of Mauss's contribution, to compare the
statement in 'Sociology' with both Durkheim's individual statements and also
his practice. If we consider only the relation between the encyclopedia entry
and Durkheim's *Rules*, we find not only the absence of a discussion of the
category of social pathology, but also the appearance of a new topic, that of
'general sociology' (which was to have an important influence on Mauss's
subsequent writing). This interest in the divisions within sociology reflects, no
doubt, the discussions in the *Année* team to classify the different fields within
the sociological project itself.

A fourth feature of Durkheim's approach of the 1890s is the attempt to
work out an order of analysis that follows a theoretically identified priority of
causal connections. Indeed, as early as his very first general statement of
sociology, his 1888 'Opening Lecture' (in Durkheim 1978:43–70), Durkheim
described the domain of sociology as being divided into morphology and
physiology which, he says, are drawn in parallel with the division in biology
between structure and function of organisms (1978:65). In *The Rules* of 1895,
Durkheim again discusses morphology and physiology (1982:57f., 135f.). The
key proposition of *The Rules* is that the facts of morphology, of the composition
of its inner social environment, 'play a preponderant role' in explanation
(ibid.:135), made up of 'firstly, the number of social units or as we have also
termed it, the "volume" of the society; and secondly, the degree of
concentration of the mass of the people, or what we have called the "dynamic
density"' (ibid.:136). Durkheim emphasises that the latter term concerns 'the
moral concentration of which physical concentration is only the auxiliary

element' (ibid.:136). In his works of the 1890s Durkheim suggests that it is through the analysis of social morphology (rather than function (physiology)) that sociology must establish causal relations. As Andrews has pointed out, Durkheim's thinking on morphology changed subtly in the late 1890s, so that collective representations could attain a relative autonomy in relation to the morphological basis of a society (1993:119). This primacy of morphology over representation, as an analytical proposition following from theoretical principles, was accepted by Mauss and formed one of the cornerstones of subsequent Durkheimian analysis (Allen provides an extensive discussion which develops the latent position to be found in Mauss: see Allen 2000:109f.).

After Durkheim's death and the interregnum of the First World War, the *Année sociologique* was restarted, and in this second series Mauss, following Durkheim's model, began again to reflect on method. His essay included here was published in the second, and indeed final, issue of the new series of the *Année* in 1927. If read from a rhetorical point of view these two texts are quite different. The text on method is transitional, and the old framework is bursting at the seams as Mauss attempted to reconstruct the sociological project in a new situation. A third set of publications – no longer called the *Année sociologique*, but the more accurately *Annales sociologiques* – was started in 1934. In its first volume was published another important strategic statement of the school, Mauss's essay 'Fragment d'un sociologie generale descriptive' with a subtitle, 'Classification et méthode d'observation des phénomènes généraux de la vie sociale dans les sociétés de type archaïques (phénomènes généraux spécifique de la vie intérieure de la société)' (in Mauss 1968–9, iii:303–54. The *Annales sociologiques* were published in parallel series A, B, C, D and E, between 1934 and 1942 (a comprehensive list of contents of the major Durkheimian journals can be found in Nandan 1977, and see Clammer 2000).

In 1927 Mauss was searching to reestablish the sociological project in the second series of the *Année*, and he admits explicitly at the beginning of the essay that he wished, in restoring the project, to 'continue a respectable tradition and not upset former and faithful readers'. However, Mauss clearly is not altogether satisfied with the organisation of the work of the school of sociology as he finds it in 1927. In particular he notes 'general sociology' and 'social morphology' are not in their proper positions (Chapter 1). The proportions are also wrong (Chapter 2). It seems as if there is a new content waiting to burst through the old formal arrangements, but Mauss is reluctant to let the process proceed. In the end Mauss appeals to his conversations with Durkheim to legitimise a fundamental change which was discussed but not developed as far back as the late 1890s. For Durkheim the overall nature of the sociological project of the first series of the *Année* could be summed up in 1909 in a formal way as follows:

I. *Social Morphology*
   The study of the geographic base of various peoples in terms of its relationships with
      their social organisation
   The study of population: its volume, its density, and its disposition on the earth
II. *Social Physiology*
   Sociology of religion
   Sociology of morality
   Sociology of law
   Economic sociology
   Linguistic sociology
   Aesthetic sociology
III. *General Sociology*

(Durkheim 1978: 83)

Durkheim says of general sociology that its object 'is to reveal the most general properties and laws of life. This is the philosophical part of the science' (Durkheim: 1978:82); and see Gane, in Pickering 2002:17–28; and Clammer 2000:30).

It is this division of work which Mauss begins to alter. His Chapter 3 of this essay 'is largely based on his conversations' with Durkheim. Indeed it is clear that the category 'general sociology' as used in the *Année sociologique* was problematic for Durkheim. In a note in volume 5 (1902) Durkheim lamented the 'extreme indeterminateness of its object' and suggested that 'general sociology could and should be something different... the role of general sociology might be to constitute the unity of all that is dissected by analysis' (in Durkheim 1982:243). Clearly, Mauss in 1927 wanted to take up the challenge Durkheim had indicated and he outlines the set of problems involved in thinking about the character of a particular society. Chapter 3 starts with a division between morphology and social physiology, and a division of the latter into the physiology of practices and the physiology of collective representations. Having discussed the advantages of this new division and arrangement, he introduces a new discussion of the category of 'concrete general sociology' (Chapter 4). The last chapter introduces issues that for Durkheim were discussed largely in relation to pathology, but which here become the concerns of 'applied sociology or politics'.

In Mauss's essay of 1927 it is clear that in effect he presents a transitional statement of the divisions within the sociological field. He presents them in this manner:

I. *Social Morphology*
   Material structures
II. *Social physiology*
   Practices
   Representations
III. *General sociology*
   Language and the symbolic
   Science

Collective ethology
Applied sociology and politics

What is striking is that Mauss begins to work out a detailed conception of general sociology that is almost completely lacking in Durkheim's formulations of the 1890s. It has been claimed that Mauss thus essentially restructures the field of sociology entirely. Karsenti, for example, controversially argues that 'relations are formed, connections established, and passages introduced which lead to a redistribution of knowledge. The latter, insofar as it no longer suffers from a foundational split, can now be seen from a unitary viewpoint and can take back the name of anthropology – although the old term has now acquired a new meaning' (Karsenti, in James and Allen 1998:80). Indeed for Karsenti, sociology in the Maussian scheme, 'has the imperative duty to fulfil itself on this basis and rediscover its place within anthropology' (ibid.).

The logic of such a development can be seen, perhaps, in the new consideration of the field published in 1934. In this version Mauss suggests that, in the final analysis, there exist only individual societies, as 'this or that closed system' (1968–9, III:306). It is this ultimate object, which can be studied only when all the individual parts of it are finally known, that can be considered the true synthetic object of 'general sociology' (ibid.). Mauss, at the same time as he emphasises the individuality of this object, was interested, he says, in defining the place of general phenomena, by which he means those that are common throughout all categories of social life (population, practices and representations). To the already given division (morphology and physiology), he suggests redefining 'general phenomena' so that it can be subdivided into its national and international aspects. To do this means, he says, abandoning the division of such a 'general sociology' into morphological and physiological facts (ibid.:312). Outlining a new set of problems, Mauss redefines basic terms such as social cohesion, social discipline and authority, and the mechanisms of their transmission (tradition, education). Then he moves on to examine intersocial relations of peace and war, and then to what he calls 'civilisation' or the contacts and commerce between individual societies. To make analysis complete, he says, there are two further divisions to examine: first the psychological, and secondly the biological. These are very quickly discussed before concluding that a complete sociological analysis would cover all the elements itemised in his plan. Thus the conception of 'general sociology' to which he has been working is outlined in four parts:

[A] general phenomena of one society – thus national
     cohesion
     discipline and authority
     transmission
     tradition
     education

[B] general phenomena of a group of societies – thus international
      war and peace
      civilisation
[C] relation to individual psychology
      collective psychology
      collective ethology
      individual psychology (with origin in the collective)
      collective psychology (with origin in the individual)
[D] relation to human biology
      biometrics
      somatic anthropology

Mauss, at the end of this discussion, suggests that the goal of a complete sociological analysis is to know:

the birth		from a triple point of view
the life	{of a society}	(i) pure sociology
the ageing		(ii) sociopsychology
and death		(iii) sociobiology

(Mauss, 1968–9, III:353)

He concludes this essay of 1934 by observing that 'it is of little use to philosophize on general sociology when one has so much to find out and to know, and when one first has so much to do in order to understand' (ibid.:354).

Bataille, Caillois, Leiris and Lévi-Strauss were attracted to Mauss's work by what they saw as a profoundly theoretical project. Bataille wrote that his own work was derived from the consideration of law and transgression in Mauss's anthropology: 'Mauss, unwilling to formulate his ideas too definitely, has merely expressed them periodically in his lecture courses' (Bataille 1990:208). Yet Mauss himself clearly avoided direct contact with Bataille's project (see Marcel 2003). Lévi-Strauss famously wrote that 'no acknowledgement of him can be proportionate to our debt, unless it comes from those who knew the man and listened to him. Only they can fully appreciate the productiveness of his thinking, which was so dense as to become opaque at times; and of his tortuous procedures, which would seem bewildering at the very moment when the most unexpected itinerary was getting to the heart of problems' (Lévi-Strauss 1987:1). It would appear, then, that Mauss would in lectures suggest more of a unified theoretical perspective than appears in his descriptive methodological writings. Recently, however, Lévi-Strauss has remarked that he did not in fact attend Mauss's lectures and that he 'only saw him a few times. It was less his person than his work that was decisive for me' (Massenzio and Lévi-Strauss 2001:423). Bataille did not attend Mauss's lectures either but depended on reports from Métraux and others (see Marcel 2003:141–2). When Bataille tried to develop a theory of horror and sacred transgression, it was pointed out to him that he had broken all the methodological rules set out by Mauss. 'If we take sociological science as it has been established by men like Durkheim, Mauss, and Robert Hertz as our reference, it is essential to stick to their methods. Otherwise, in order to clear up any ambiguity, we have to stop calling ourselves "sociologists" ' (Leiris, in Hollier 1988:355).

If Mauss seems to have moved very strongly, under pressure from Durkheim, in the direction of anthropology – whether it be called ethnology or ethnography – and away from sociology, Mauss even says, later, 'I have never been a militant of sociology' (in Besnard 1983:142). He was certainly willing to commit himself to political analysis as such in a way that Durkheim rarely was. But Mauss kept this side of his writing quite distinct and separate from his academic work which focused precisely on anthropological themes. Thus with the publication of his political writings, it is clear that Mauss had very specific criticisms of Marxism and communism, particularly Soviet communism (see his 'A Sociological Assessment of Bolshevism' in Gane 1992:165–215). It seems certain that Mauss followed the Soviet experience closely because he thought that in some way a key element of Durkheimian sociology was being put to the test. He said, 'the closeness of Durkheim's theory and the practice of the Soviets should be emphasised' (in Gane 1992:172). His critique of the Soviet experience was a bitter one, and was not only based on methodological principles. Mauss also drew out lessons which he expressed in terms of practical principles. Central to Mauss's vision is that 'Durkheim's hypotheses about the moral and economic value of the professional group emerge further confirmed from the Bolshevik test. The Soviets failed because they undermined and destroyed this primordial organisational element' (ibid.:191). But Mauss also goes further than Durkheim and suggests that every social revolution 'will take a national character' (ibid.:187); and as for political practice and law, Mauss concludes that violence does not create and neither does law create, new institutions: 'law does not create, it sanctions' (ibid.:199). The conception of method that comes through this critique of communism is that the Marxists are 'enslaved by the old doctrine: they thought that political power, the law, the decree, so long as it was they who promulgated them, could forge the new society. Profound mistake!' (ibid.:200).

Thus, like Durkheim, Mauss did not believe the new socialist society would be a return to a simpler form, one without a state, without a market and without money (ibid.:188–9). Modern societies do not return to less organisation, or to gift exchange. They become more organised, not less organised. Thus, the whole attempt to use Mauss to provide a theory of a new post-capitalist society based on symbolic exchange would not have been acceptable to Mauss himself. Indeed, in his letters on fascism written at the end of the 1930s he stresses the backward nature of secret sects which structurally could be found in communism and fascism (ibid.:213), and in an extraordinary piece of self-criticism suggested apropos fascism: 'we did not put our minds to this return of primitivism. We were satisfied with a few allusions to crowd states, when something quite different was at stake' (ibid.:214).

These political observations drawn from Mauss's polemical writings can be compared instructively with those pages that appear on law, politics and the nation in his academic publications. What is clear is that Mauss rarely makes the mistake committed by Bataille of applying the criteria appropriate to segmental and polysegmental societies to those of a quite different, national or organic type, even when it is a question of what he calls 'primitivism'. If, as has been claimed, Durkheim was the principal founder of modern French sociology and can be thought of as its Darwin, and Marcel Mauss, Durkheim's nephew, reconstructed this science in the way that Mendel relates to Darwin – that is, as someone who continues the first steps with important, even decisive, second steps – the intellectual outcome of this tradition is still to be worked out.

References

Allen, N. 2000 *Categories and Classification: Maussian Reflections on the Social*, Oxford: Berghahn.

Andrews, H. 1993 'Durkheim and Social Morphology', in S. Turner (ed.) *Emile Durkheim: Sociologist and Moralist*, London: Routledge.

Bataille, G. 1990 *Literature and Evil*, London: Marion Boyars.

Baudrillard, J. 1993 *Symbolic Exchange and Death*, London: Sage.

Baudrillard, J. 2002 *Impossible Exchange*. London: Verso.

Besnard, P. (ed.) 1983 The *Sociological Domain. The Durkheimians and the Founding of French sociology*, Cambridge: Cambridge University Press.

Borlandi, M. and Mucchielli, L. (eds) *La Sociologie et sa Méthode*, Paris: L'Harmattan.

Bourdieu, P. 2000 *Pascalian Mediations*, Cambridge: Polity.

Caillé, A. 1994 *Don, Intérêt et désintéessement. Bourdieu, Mauss, Platon et quelques autres*, Paris: La Découverte.

Carrithers, M., Collins, S. and Lukes, S. (eds) 1985 *The Category of the Person: Anthropology, Philosophy, History*, Cambridge: Cambridge University Press.

Cazeneuve, J. 1968 *Sociologie de Marcel Mauss*, Paris: Presses Universitaires de France.

Clammer, J. 2000 'The categories of knowledge in the Année Sociologique', *Durkheimian Studies*, n.s., 6:27–42.

Derrida, J. 1992 *Given Time: 1. Counterfeit Money*, Chicago: University of Chicago Press.

Dubar, C. 1975 'The methodology of Marcel Mauss', in *The Graduate Faculty Journal of Sociology*, New School for Social Research, NY, 1,1:1–12.

Durkheim, E. 1964 *The Division of Labour in Society*, London: Collier-Macmillan.

Durkheim, E. 1978 *On Institutional Analysis*, Chicago: University of Chicago Press.

Durkheim, E. 1982 *The Rules of Sociological Method and Selected Texts on Sociology and its Method*, London: Macmillan.

Durkheim. E. 1998 *Lettres à Marcel Mauss*, Paris: Presses Universitaires de France.

Durkheim E. and Mauss, M.1963 *Primitive Classification*, Chicago: University of Chicago Press.

Fournier, M. 1994 *Marcel Mauss*, Paris: Fayard.

Gane, M. 1988 *On Durkheim's Rules of Sociological Method*, London: Routledge.

Gane, M. (ed) 1992 *The Radical Sociology of Durkheim and Mauss*, London: Routledge.

Gane, M. 2003 *French Social Theory*, London: Sage.

Genosko, G. 1998 *Undisciplined Theory*, London: Routledge.

Godelier, M. 1999 *The Enigma of the Gift*, Oxford: Polity.

Hamilton, P. (ed.) 1990. *Emile Durkheim: Critical Assessments*, 4 vols. London: Routledge.

Heilbron, J. 1985 'Les métamorphoses du durkheimisme, 1920-1940', in: *Revue Française de Sociologie*, 26:203–37.

Hollier, D. (ed.) 1988 *The College of Sociology 1937–39*, Minneapolis: University of Minnesota Press.

Hubert, H. and Mauss, M. 1964 *Sacrifice: Its Nature and Functions*, London: Cohen and West.

James, W. and Allen, N. (eds) 1998 *Marcel Mauss: A Centenary Tribute*, Oxford: Berghahn Books.

Johnson, C. 1997 'Anthropology and sociology: from Mauss to Lévi-Strauss', *Modern and Contemporary France*, 5, 4:421–31.

Johnson, C. 2003 *Claude Lévi-Strauss: The Formative Years*, Cambridge: Cambridge University Press.

Karsenti, B. 1994 *Marcel Mauss: Le Fait Social Total*, Paris: Presses Universitaires de France.

Karsenti, B. 1997 *L'Homme Total. Sociologie, Anthropologie et Philosophie chez Marcel Mauss*, Paris: Presses Universitaires de France.

Lévi-Strauss, C. 1987 *Introduction to the Work of Marcel Mauss*. London: Routledge and Kegan Paul.

Marcel, J.-C. 2003 'Bataille and Mauss: a dialogue of the deaf?' in: *Economy and Society*, 32, 1:141–52.

Massenzio, M. and Lévi-Strauss, C. 2001. 'An Interview with Claude Lévi-Strauss', *Current Anthropology*, 42, 1:419–25.

Mauss, M. 1947 *Manuel d'Ethnographie*, Paris: Payot.

Mauss, M. 1966 *The Gift*, Foreword by E. E. Evans-Pritchard, London: Cohen and West.

Mauss, M. 1968 *Sociologie et Anthropologie*, Paris: Presses Universitaires de France.

Mauss, M. 1968–9 *Oeuvres*, 3 vols. Paris: Minuit.

Mauss, M. 1979 *Sociology and Psychology: Essays*, London: Routledge and Kegan Paul. [This is a translation of parts 3, 4, 5 and 6 of Mauss 1968]

Mauss, M. 1990 *The Gift*, Foreword by M. Douglas, London: Routledge.

Mauss, M. 1997 *Ecrits Politiques*, Paris: Fayard.

Mauss, M. 1999 'Paul Fauconnet', *Durkheimian Studies*, n.s., 5: 24–8.

Mauss, M. 2001 'Contribution to discussion: "Le genre féminin deans les langues européenes" ', *Durkhiemian Studies*, n.s., 7:1–5.

Mauss, M. 2003 *On Prayer*, Oxford: Durkheim Press/Berghahn Books.

Mauss, M. and Beuchat, H. 1979 *Seasonal Variations of the Eskimo: A Study in Social Morphology*, London: Routledge and Kegan Paul.

Mauss, M. and Hubert, H. 1972 *A General Theory of Magic*, London: Routledge and Kegan Paul.

Merleau-Ponty, M. 1964 *Signs*. Evanston, Ill.: Northwestern University Press.

Mucchielli, L. 1998 *La Découverte du Social*, Paris: Editions La Découverte.

Nandan, Y. 1977 *The Durkheim School: A Systematic and Comprehensive Bibliography*, London: Greenwood.

Pickering, W.S.F. (ed.) 2002 *Durkheim Today*, Oxford: Berghahn Books.

Richman, M. 1995 'The sacred group: A Durkheimian perspective on the Collège de Sociologie', *Bataille: Writing the Sacred*, London: Routledge.

Richman, M. 1997 'Rejection and renewal: Durkheim and the 20th century', *Modern and Contemporary France*, 5, 4:409–19.

Richman, M. 2002 *Sacred Revolution: Durkheim and the Collège de Sociologie*, Minneapolis: University of Minnesota Press.
Richman, M. 2003 'Myth, power and the sacred: anti-utilitarianism in the Collège de Sociologie, 1937–9', *Economy and Society*, 32,1:29–47.
Strenski, I. 1997 *Durkheim and the Jews of France*, Chicago: University of Chicago Press.
Tarot, C. 1999 *De Durkheim à Mauss: l'Invention du Symbolique*, Paris: la Découverte.
Tollebeek, J. 2002 'The archive: the panoptic utopia of the historian', in F. Musarra, B. Van Den Bossche, K. Du Pont, N. Dupre, R. Gennaro and S. Vanvolsem (eds), *Eco in Fabula: Umberto Eco in the Humanities*, Leuven: Leuven University Press, pp. 339–55.
Turner, S. (ed.) 1993 *Emile Durkheim: Sociologist and Moralist*, London: Routledge.

Marcel Mauss

(in collaboration with Paul Fauconnet)

SOCIOLOGY

First published in French in 1901 as 'Sociologie', in *La grande encyclopédie*, 30, pp. 165–76.

Sociology is a word created by Auguste Comte to designate the science of societies. Though the word was formed from a Latin root and a Greek ending, and for that reason purists have long refused to recognise it, it has today been naturalised in all the European languages. We shall attempt to determine successively the subject-matter of sociology and the method which it employs. Then we shall indicate the principal divisions of the science which is being constituted under this name.

The reader will see without difficulty that we are inspired directly by the ideas expressed by Durkheim in his different writings. If we adopt them, moreover, we do so not only because they appear to us to be justified on theoretical grounds, but also because they seem to us to express the principles of which the various social sciences tend to become increasingly conscious in the course of their development.

I. The Subject-matter of Sociology

Because sociology is of recent origin and has hardly emerged from the philosophical phase, it still happens that its possibility can be disputed. All of the metaphysical traditions which view man as a being apart, outside of nature, and which see in his behaviour facts which are absolutely different from natural facts, resist the progress of sociological thought. The sociologist, however, does not need to justify his researches by any philosophical argument. Science must do its work from the moment when it perceives the possibility, and no philosophical arguments, even traditional ones, can constitute objections to the legitimacy of its proceedings. If, moreover, as seems probable, the scientific study of societies renders necessary a different conception of human nature, the task for philosophy is to put itself in harmony with science, insofar as the latter obtains results. Science, however, has no concern to foresee or to avoid the remote consequences of its discoveries.

The only postulate of sociology is simply that the facts labelled 'social' are in nature, that is, are subject to the principles of order and of universal determinism, and are therefore intelligible. This hypothesis is not the fruit of metaphysical speculations; it results from a generalisation which seems perfectly legitimate. This hypothesis, principle of all science, has successively been extended to all fields, even to those which seemed most to escape its grasp. It is therefore rational to suppose that the social field – if it is a field which merits being thus labelled – does not form an exception. It is not up to the sociologist to demonstrate that social phenomena are subject to this law; the burden is on the adversary of sociology to provide proof to the contrary. A priori, one must admit that whatever has been found to be true of physical, biological and psychic facts is also true of social facts. Only a definitive defeat could ruin this logical presumption. Henceforth, this defeat is no longer to be feared. It is no longer possible to say that the science of sociology is still entirely to be constructed. We do not dream of exaggerating the importance of the results which the science has achieved; nevertheless, despite all the scepticisms, it does exist and it does progress. It raises definite problems and it more or less perceives solutions. The more it enters into contact with the facts and the more it sees the emergence of previously unsuspected regularities and relationships, far more precise than could have initially been supposed, the stronger the feeling becomes that the observer is in the presence of a natural order, whose existence can no longer be put in doubt except by philosophers who are remote from the reality they claim to talk about.

Although one must admit without preliminary examination that the facts called 'social' are natural, intelligible, and therefore objects of science, it is still necessary that facts exist which can properly be characterised by this adjective. In order for a new science to be constituted, it is sufficient is necessary, on the one hand, that it be involved with an order of facts clearly distinct from those facts which are the concern of the other sciences; on the other hand, these facts must be susceptible of being immediately related to one another, and explained by one another, without any need to intercalate some other kind of facts. Any science which cannot explain the facts constituting its subject-matter except by resorting to another science confounds itself with this latter. Does sociology satisfy this double condition?

Concerning the Phenomenon of the Social

First, are there facts which are specifically social? This is still commonly denied, and among those who deny it are even to be found some thinkers who claim to do sociological work. The example of Tarde is characteristic. For him, 'social' facts are nothing but ideas or individual sentiments which have been propagated by imitation. They have, therefore, no specific character, because a phenomenon[1] does not change its nature by being more or less frequently repeated. For the moment we need not discuss this theory, but we must state that, if it is well founded, then sociology is not distinguished from individual psychology, that is, the subject-matter for a sociology properly so called is lacking. The same conclusion follows, whatever be the theory, immediately the specific quality of social facts is denied. From this the reader will perceive the importance of the question that we are examining.

One initial fact is constant: societies, that is, aggregations of human beings, exist. Among these aggregations some are durable, like nations; others are ephemeral, like crowds; some are very large, like the great churches; others are very tiny, like the family when it is reduced to the two spouses. However, whatever may be the sise and form of these groups and of others that could be enumerated – class, tribe, occupational group, caste, commune – one characteristic possessed by all of them is that they are formed by a plurality of individual conscious minds, acting and reacting upon one another. By the presence of these actions and reactions, these *interactions*, one recognises societies. The question is whether, among the phenomena which occur within these groups, there are any which manifest the nature of the group as a group, and not merely the nature of the individuals who compose them, in other words, the general attributes of humanity. Are there phenomena which are what they are because the group is what it is? On this condition, and on this condition only, there will be a sociology rightly so called, for then there will be a life of society as distinct from that led by the individuals or, rather, distinct from the life they would lead if they lived in isolation.

Phenomena exhibiting these characteristics truly exist, the only question is to discover them. In fact, it is not the case that everything that occurs in a social group is a manifestation of the life of the group as such, and is therefore social, any more than everything which occurs in an organism is properly biological. Apart from the local and accidental perturbations determined by environmental causes, consider normal events, regularly repeated, which involve all the members of the group without exception. These can perfectly well lack the character of social facts. For example, all individuals, with the exception of invalids, perform their organic functions in observably identical conditions; the same is true of psychological functions. Phenomena of sensation, representation, reaction or inhibition are the same among all the members of the group. Among all of them the phenomena are subject to the very laws which are studied by psychology. No one, however, would dream of placing these phenomena in the category of social facts, despite their generality. The fact is they are not in any way related to the nature of the group, but instead derive from the organic and psychic nature of the individual. Moreover they are identical, whatever the group to which the individual belongs. If isolated humans were conceivable, it might be said that the phenomena would be just the same apart from all that is social. If then the facts for which societies serve as a theatre are only to be distinguished from one another by the degree of their generality, there would be none that could be considered as the unique manifestations of social life, and which in consequence could form the subject-matter of sociology.

Nevertheless, the existence of such phenomena is so obvious that it was remarked on by observers who never dreamt of constituting a sociology. It has often been noted that a crowd or an assembly does not feel, does not think, and does not act as would the separate individuals who constitute them; that the most diverse groups – a family, a corporation, a nation – have a 'spirit', a character, and habits, as individuals have theirs. In all these cases, observers consequently feel that the group, crowd or society has truly a unique nature, which determines certain manners of feeling, thinking and acting by the individuals, and that the individuals would have neither the same tendencies, nor the same habits, nor the same prejudices, if they had lived in other human groups. This conclusion may be generalised. Between the ideas that he has and the acts that an isolated individual would do, on the one hand, and collective manifestations on the other hand, there exists such an abyss that these latter should be related to a new *nature*, to forces *sui generis*, for otherwise they would remain incomprehensible.

Take, for example, manifestations in the economic life of modern Western societies: the industrial production of goods, an extreme division of labour, international exchange, capital structures, money, credit, rent, interest, wages, etc. Consider the large number of notions, institutions and habits, presupposed in the simplest acts of a merchant or of a worker who seeks to earn his living: the obvious fact is that neither of them have created the forms which their activity necessarily takes; neither of them invented credit, interest, wages, exchange or money. All that can be attributed to each of them is a general tendency to procure the food he needs and to protect himself against bad weather, as well as for example, the inclination for enterprise, profit etc. Even those sentiments which seem to be wholly spontaneous – the love of work, thrift, extravagance – are, in reality, the product of social culture, inasmuch as they do not appear among certain peoples and vary infinitely within a single society, according to the social strata of the population. By themselves, these needs would necessitate for their satisfaction a small number of very simple acts, that contrast in the most pronounced fashion with the very complex forms in which economic man casts his behaviour today. And it is not only the complexity of these forms that testify to their extra-individual origin, but also and particularly the manner in which they impose themselves upon the individual. The latter is more or less obliged to conform with them. Sometimes one is constrained by the law itself or by custom, which is no less imperative than the law. Thus, not long ago, the manufacturer was obliged to make products of specified measures and quality; even now he is subject to all kinds of regulations; and no one can refuse to receive in payment legal tender at its legal value. Sometimes it is the force of things upon which the individual comes to grief when he tries to rebel against them. Thus, the merchant who would renounce credit, the producer who would consume his own products, in a word, the worker who would recreate entirely by himself the rules of his economic activity, will witness themselves condemned to inevitable ruin.

Language is another fact whose social character appears clearly. By usage and study a child learns a language whose vocabulary and syntax are many centuries old and whose origins are unknown, which he consequently receives completely fashioned and which he is expected to accept and to use without considerable variations. In vain would he attempt to create an original language. Not only would he end by awkwardly imitating some other existing idiom, but in addition such a language would not serve to express his thought. It would condemn him to isolation and a kind of intellectual death. The simple fact of parting from rules and from traditional usages most generally encounters extremely vigorous resistances from opinion. For a language is not only a system of words; it has a particular genius and it implies a certain manner of perceiving, analysing and coordination. Consequently, through the language, it is the principal forms of our thought that are imposed upon us by the collectivity.

It might seem that matrimonial and domestic relations are necessarily what they are by virtue of human nature, and that to explain them it would be sufficient to recall some very general organic and psychological properties of the human individual. However, on the one hand, historical observation teaches us that the types of marriages and of families have been and still are extremely numerous and varied; it reveals to us the sometimes extraordinary complication of the forms of marriage and of the domestic relations. And, on the other hand, we know that domestic relations are not exclusively affective, that between us and relatives whom we may not know, there exist juridical bonds which have come into being without our consent and without our knowledge. We know also that marriage is not only a pairing, that on the man who marries a woman law and customs impose prescribed acts, a complicated procedure. Manifestly, neither the man's organic tendencies to pair off or to procreate, nor even the sentiments of sexual jealousy or paternal tenderness that might be gratuitously imputed to him, can in any degree explain either the complexity or, more particularly, the obligatory character of matrimonial and domestic mores.

Likewise, the very general religious sentiments customarily attributed to man and even to animals – respect and fear of superior beings, anguish about infinity – could engender only very simple and very indeterminate religious acts. Each man, under the rule of these emotions, would envisage superior beings in his own fashion and manifest his sentiments to them as seems to him appropriate. So simple, indeterminate and individual a religion has never existed. The believer accepts dogmas and acts according to rites which are both extremely complicated and which have, moreover, been instilled in him from outside by the Church, or the religious group to which he belongs. In general, he knows these dogmas and rites most imperfectly, and his religious life consists essentially in a distant participation in beliefs and acts of men who are specially charged with knowing the sacred things and with entering into rapport with them. Furthermore, these men did not invent the dogmas or the rites; they were taught them by tradition, and are particularly watchful to preserve them from any alteration. Thus, the individual sentiments of the faithful do not explain either the complex system of ideas [*représentations*] and practices which constitute a religion or the authority by which these manners of thought and acting are imposed on all the members of the Church.

The forms governing the development of the affective, intellectual and active life of the individual pre-exist him, just as they will survive him. It is because he is a man, that he eats, thinks, amuses himself etc., but if he is influenced to act by tendencies he shares with all men, the precise forms taken by his behaviour at each moment of history depend upon totally different conditions which vary from one society to another and change through time within a single society – the totality of collective habits. These habits are of various kinds. Some of them invite reflection because of their own importance. People are aware of these and preserve them in written or oral formulae, which express how the group is in the habit of acting, and how it demands that its members act. These imperative formulae are rules of law, maxims of morality, precepts of ritual, articles of dogma etc. Other habits remain unexpressed and diffuse, more or less unconscious. Customs, mores and popular superstitions are observed without knowing that one is bound by them, or even precisely what they consist of. The nature of the phenomenon in the two cases, however, is the same. It is always a matter of acting or thinking, consecrated by tradition, and which is imposed by society upon the individual. These collective habits and the unending transformations they undergo are the proper subject-matter of sociology.

Moreover, it is now possible to prove directly that these collective habits are the manifestations of the life of the group as a group. The comparative history of law and of religions, has popularised the idea that some institutions form a system with other institutions, and that the former cannot be transformed without the latter being equally transformed. For example, we know that there are links between totemism and exogamy, and between both these practices and the organisation of the clan; we know that the system of patriarchal power is related to the regime of the city, etc. In a general fashion, historians have adopted the habit of showing the interrelations which different institutions sustain in a single period, and of not isolating an institution from the milieu wherein it has appeared. Finally, there is an increasing trend to look to the properties of a social milieu (its volume, density, mode of composition etc.), for the explanation of the general phenomena appearing therein. It might show, for example, what are the profound modifications brought by urban agglomeration to an agricultural civilisation, or how the form of the habitat conditions domestic organisation. If, then, institutions depend one upon another and all depend on the constitution of the social group, obviously it is because they express the latter. This *interdependence* of phenomena would be inexplicable if they were the products of individual and more or less capricious volitions; on the other hand, they can be explained if they are the products of impersonal forces which dominate individuals themselves.

Another proof can be drawn from the study of statistics. We know that the figures which express the numbers of marriages, births, suicides and crimes in a society are remarkably constant or that, if they vary, they do so not by sudden and irregular jumps, but generally in a slow and orderly fashion. Their constancy and their regularity are at least equal to those of phenomena which, like mortality, depend particularly upon physical causes. Manifestly, the causes which impel some particular individual into marriage or crime are entirely individual and accidental; these are not, therefore, the causes that can explain the rates of marriage or crime in a given society. We must admit the existence of certain social states, entirely different from purely individual states, which condition marriage and criminality. For example, one cannot understand why the level of suicide should be uniformly higher in Protestant societies than in Catholic societies or in the commercial world rather than in the agricultural world, unless one admits that a collective tendency to suicide manifests itself in Protestant milieux or in commercial milieux, by virtue of their very organisation.

There are, then, specifically social phenomena, distinct from those studied by the other sciences which deal with man, for example, psychology. These phenomena constitute the subject-matter of sociology. It is not sufficient, however, to have established their existence by a certain number of examples and by general considerations. We still wish to know the sign by which they can be distinguished in such a way as neither to risk allowing some phenomena to escape nor to hazard confusing them with phenomena belonging to other sciences. In the light of what has been said above, the social nature has precisely the characteristic of being, as it were, superadded to individual nature; it is expressed by ideas or acts which, even though we contribute to produce them, are entirely imposed upon us from outside. The problem is to discover this sign of externality.

In a great number of cases, the obligatory character which marks the social ways of acting and thinking is the best criterion one could desire. Whether deep in the heart or expressed in legal formulae, whether obeyed spontaneously or instilled by way of constraint, a multitude of legal, religious and moral rules are rigorously obligatory. The majority of individuals obey them; even those who violate them know that they have failed in an obligation; and, in any case, society reminds them of the obligatory character of its order by inflicting sanctions upon them. Whatever be the nature and the intensity of the sanction – excommunication or death, damages or imprisonment, public disgrace, rebuke, merely a reputation for eccentricity – in varying degrees and under diverse forms – the phenomenon is always the same: the group protests against the violation of the collective rules of thought and action. This protest can have only one meaning: the ways of thinking and acting which the group imposes are the proper ways of thinking and acting. Society does not tolerate any exemption from them, because it sees in them the manifestations of its personality: it sees that exemption from them causes this personality to be diminished or destroyed. Moreover, if the rules of thought and action did not have a social origin, where could they come from? A rule to which an individual believes himself subject, cannot be that individual's work, because every obligation implies an authority which is superior to the obligated subject, and which inspires in him respect, the essential element in the sentiment of obligation. If, then, the intervention of supernatural beings is excluded, only one source of obligation above and beyond the individual can be found, namely, society, or rather the series of societies of which the individual is a member.

We have, therefore, an easily recognisable gathering [*ensemble*] of social phenomena of prime importance, because law, morality and religion form a notable part of social life. Indeed, in primitive societies hardly any collective manifestations do not fall within one or the other of these categories. In these societies, humans do not, as it were, have their own thought or activity; language, economic operations, even clothing, often take on a religious character, and as a consequence, they are obligatory. In advanced societies, however, there is a great number of cases where social pressure does not make itself felt under the explicit form of obligation. In economic, juristic, indeed even religious matters, the individual seems largely autonomous. This is not to say that all coercion is absent; we have shown above the aspects under which it is manifest in the economic and linguistic orders, and how far it is from being the case that the individual is free in these matters to act in his own way. Meanwhile, there is no proclaimed obligation, no defined sanctions; in principle, innovation and self-exemption are not proscribed. It is necessary, therefore, to seek another criterion which allows us to distinguish those habits whose special nature is no less incontestable, although it is less immediately apparent.

It is incontestable in fact because each individual finds them already formed, and, as it were, *instituted*, because he is not their author, but receives them from outside – they are thus *pre-established*. Whether or not the individual is forbidden to depart from them, they already exist at the moment when he collects his thoughts to know how he should act. What they present him with are models of behaviour. In addition, one sees them, as it were, at a particular moment penetrating him from outside. In the majority of cases, this penetration is accomplished through education, either general or special. In this way each generation receives from its predecessor its precepts of morality, its rules of customary politeness, its language, and its fundamental tastes, precisely as each worker receives from his predecessors the rules of his occupational techniques. Education is precisely the operation through which, in each of us, the social being is superadded to the individual being, the moral being to the animal being. Thanks to this procedure, the infant is rapidly socialised. These observations supply us with a characteristic of the social fact much more general than the one mentioned above. Social ways of acting and thinking are all those that the individual finds pre-established, and that are most generally transmitted by education.

It would be good if a special word were to designate these special facts, and it seems that the word *institutions* would be the most appropriate. What, in fact, is an institution if not a grouping of acts and ideas already instituted which individuals find before them and which more or less imposes itself upon them? There is no reason for the ordinary practice of reserving this expression exclusively for fundamental social arrangements. By institutions, therefore, we understand customs and fashions, prejudices and superstitions, just as much as political constitutions or essential legal organisations, because all of these phenomena are of the same nature and differ from one another only in degree. In summary, an institution is in the social order what function is in the biological order, and just as the science of life is a science of vital functions, so the science of society is the science of institutions thus defined.

However, it will be urged, an institution is of the past. By definition, it is something fixed, not something living. At every point of time, societies are producing novelties, from the almost daily variations in style to the great political and moral revolutions. All these changes, however, are always varying degrees of modifications of existing institutions. Revolutions have never consisted in the sudden and integral substitution of a new order for the established order; always they are, and can only be, more or less rapid, more or less complete, transformations. Nothing comes from nothing: new institutions can only be created from old ones, because the latter are the only ones that exist. Consequently, in order for our definition to embrace all that is to be defined, it is sufficient that we do not limit ourselves to a narrowly static formula, that we do not restrain sociology to the study of the supposedly immobile institution. Conceived in this way, an institution is in reality merely an abstraction. True institutions live, that is, change incessantly; the rules of action are neither understood nor applied in the same manner at successive moments, even though the formulae in which they are expressed remain literally the same. It is, then, living institutions, as they are formed, function, and are transformed at different moments, which constitute specifically social phenomena, the subject-matter of sociology.

The only facts which could with some reason be regarded as social and which, nevertheless, are with difficulty incorporated in the definition of institutions, are those which appear in societies without institutions. The only societies without institutions, however, are social aggregations which are either highly unstable and ephemeral, for example, crowds, or else those which are in the process of formation. We may say of both that they are still not societies as such, but only societies in the process of becoming, with this difference: some of them are destined to reach the end-point of their development and to achieve their social nature, whereas others disappear before arriving at their definitive constitution. At this point we are on the boundaries which separate the social field from lower fields.[2] The phenomena in question are on the way to becoming social but are not yet social. It is, therefore, not surprising that they do not fit exactly in the frameworks of any science. Sociology, of course, should not reject all interest in them, but they do not constitute its proper object. Moreover, we have not sought in the foregoing analysis to discover a complete and definitive definition of all social phenomena. It is enough to have shown that facts do exist which merit being so labelled, and to have indicated some signs by which the more important among them can be recognised. For these criteria, the future will most certainly substitute others which are less defective.

On Sociological Explanation

Sociology, therefore, has its proper subject-matter, since there are facts which are properly social. It remains for us to see whether it satisfies the second of the conditions which we have indicated, that is, whether there exists a sociological mode of explanation that is not confused with any other mode. The first mode of explanation which was methodically applied to these phenomena is the one which has long been in use in what is usually called the philosophy of history. The philosophy of history was in fact the form of sociological speculation immediately antecedent to sociology properly so called. Sociology was born from the philosophy of history. Comte was the immediate successor of Condorcet, and himself constructed a philosophy of history rather than making any sociological discoveries. What characterises the philosophical explanation is its assumption that man, humanity in general, is predisposed by his nature to a particular path of development, whose whole orientation it attempts to discover by a summary investigation of historical facts. As a matter of principle and method, details are neglected in order to concentrate on the most general lines. No effort is made to explain why such and such an institution is encountered in such and such a type of society at a particular epoch in its development. The aim is only to find what is the goal towards which humanity directs itself and to mark the stages that one deems to have been necessary to it in order to approach this goal.

There is no point in demonstrating the insufficiency of such an explanation. Not only does it arbitrarily leave aside the greater part of historical reality but, because it is no longer possible today to maintain that humanity follows a single path and develops in a single direction, all these systems are, by that fact alone, deprived of any foundation. But the explanations still to be found today in certain sociological doctrines, however, do not greatly differ from the foregoing, save perhaps in appearance. On the assumption that society is only formed of individuals, it is in the nature of the individual that such theorists seek the determining causes by means of which they will endeavour to explain social facts. For example, Spencer and Tarde proceed in this fashion. Spencer devotes nearly all the first volume of his *Sociology* to the study of primitive man, in his physical, emotional and intellectual aspects. It is by drawing on the properties of this primitive man that he explains the social institutions observed among the oldest peoples and the most savage peoples, institutions which are transformed in the course of history, according to very general *laws of evolution*. Tarde sees the supreme principles of sociology in the *laws of imitation*. Social phenomena are modes of action that are generally useful, invented by certain individuals and imitated by all the others. The same procedure of explanation may be found in certain special sciences which are or should be sociological.

Thus, the classical economists find, in the individual nature of *homo oeconomicus*, the principles of an adequate explanation of all economic facts: since man always seeks the greatest advantage at the price of the least cost, the economic relations necessarily should be such and such. Likewise, the theorists of natural law search for the juristic and moral characteristics of human nature, and in these theorists' eyes, juristic institutions are more or less successful attempts to satisfy the demands of that nature. Man becomes conscious of himself step by step, and positive laws are the approximate realisations of the law which he bears within himself.

The insufficiency of these solutions clearly appears as soon as one has recognised that there exist social facts, social realities, that is, as soon as the specific subject-matter of sociology has been distinguished. If in fact social phenomena are the manifestations of the life of groups as groups, they are much too complex to be explained by any considerations relating to human nature in general. As an example, let us once more consider the institutions of marriage and the family. Sexual relationships are subject to very complicated rules; familial organisation, while very stable in a single society, varies greatly from one society to another. In addition, it is closely linked with political organisation and with economic organisation, both of which again present characteristic differences in different societies. If these are the social phenomena to be explained, some precise problems arise. How have the different matrimonial and domestic systems been formed? Can the systems be linked one to another, and can subsequent forms be distinguished from antecedent ones, the former appearing as the product of the transformation of the latter? If that is possible, how are these transformations to be explained, and what are their conditions? How do the formations of familial organisation affect political and economic organisations? Besides, once some particular domestic regime is constituted, how does it function? The sociologists who seek to rely wholly upon individual psychology alone for their principle of explanation cannot provide any answers to these questions. In fact, they cannot explain these institutions which are so multiple and so various, except by linking them with some very general components of the individual's organic-psychic constitution: sexual instinct, tendency to the exclusive and jealous possession of a single female, maternal and paternal love, horror of sexual relations between kin, etc. But such explanations are suspect first of all from the purely philosophical point of view. They consist quite simply in attributing to man the sentiments which his behaviour manifests, whereas it is precisely these sentiments that need to be explained. In substance this amounts to explaining a phenomenon by the occult virtues of substances, for example, flame by phlogiston, and the fall of bodies by their heaviness. Moreover, they do not establish any precise relationship of coexistence or succession between phenomena, but arbitrarily isolate them and present them outside time and space, detached from any definite milieu. Even supposing one takes as an explanation of monogamy the affirmation that this matrimonial regime satisfies human instincts better than another, or reconciles the two spouses' liberty and dignity better than another regime, the question remains, why this regime appears in certain societies rather than in others, and at this moment and not at some other point in a society's development. Thirdly, the essential properties of human nature are the same everywhere, apart from nuances and differences of degree. How can they explain the highly varied forms which each institution has successively taken? Paternal and maternal love and the sentiments of filial affection are virtually identical among primitive and civilised peoples; but what a gap there is between the primitive organisation of the family and its present state, and, between these extremes, how many changes have occurred! Finally, man's indeterminate tendencies cannot explain forms so precise and so complex as those in which historical realities always appear. The egoism which can impel man to appropriate useful things is not the source of those complicated rules which at every period of history constitute the law of property, rules relating to title and possession, to movables and immovables, to easements, etc. And yet, the law of property *in abstracto* does not exist. What does exist is the law of property as it was or is now organised, in contemporary France or in ancient Rome, with the multitude of principles which determine it. Conceived of along such lines, sociology can attain in this fashion only the most highly general outlines, almost impossible to grasp by reason of the indeterminate quality of institutions. If such principles are adopted, one has to admit that the greatest part of social reality – all the detail of institutions – remains unexplained and inexplicable. Only the phenomena which are determined by human nature in general, always fundamentally identical in its base, will be natural and intelligible; all the particular traits which impart to institutions their specificity in accord with time and place, everything which distinguishes social individualities, will be regarded as artificial and accidental. It will be seen either as the result of fortuitous inventions, or as the products of the individual activity of legislators, of powerful men deliberately directing societies toward ends foreseen by them. The effect is therefore to put outside of science, as being non-intelligible, all the highly determined institutions, that is, social facts themselves, the proper objects of sociological science. In other words, along with the definite object of a social science, social science itself is annihilated, and one has to be satisfied with asking from philosophy and psychology some very general indications on the destinies of man living in society.

To these explanations characterised by their extreme generality, we may oppose what may properly be termed historical explanations. We do not suggest that history has known no others, but those we shall discuss are found exclusively among the historians. Obliged by the very conditions of his work to devote himself exclusively to one society and to one specific period, familiar with the spirit, the language, the characteristics particular to that society and that era, the historian naturally has a tendency to see in phenomena which concern him only those features which distinguish one from another, what gives them in each isolated case their own physiognomy – in a word, what renders them non-comparable. Seeking to discover the mentality of the peoples whose history he studies, he is inclined to accuse all those who have not, like himself, lived in intimacy with these peoples of being unintelligent and incompetent. As a consequence, he is led to distrust all comparison and all generalisation. When he studies an institution, its most individual characteristics are what attract his attention, those features of the institution which are due to the particular circumstances in which it was established or modified, and the institution appears to him as inseparable from these circumstances. For example, the patriarchal family will be an essentially Roman thing; feudalism will be an institution specific to our medieval societies, etc. From this point of view, institutions can only be considered as local and accidental combinations which depend upon equally local and accidental conditions. While the philosophers and the psychologists offer us theories allegedly valid for all of humanity, the only explanations which the historians believe to be possible are applicable only to a particular society, considered at some precise moment in its evolution. It is not admitted that there may be general causes acting everywhere, the search for which could be usefully undertaken; the historian takes upon himself the task of linking particular events to other particular events. In reality, he assumes in the facts both intimate diversity and also an infinite contingency.

To this narrowly historical method of explanation of social facts, it is necessary first to oppose the lessons owed to the comparative method. Nowadays the comparative history of religions, of legal systems, and of customs has revealed the existence of institutions which are incontestably identical among the most different peoples. Given these concordances, the imitation of one society by the others could not, even conceivably, be assigned as a cause. It is also impossible to consider them as fortuitous. Obviously, similar institutions cannot have local and accidental causes in a savage people, and other causes equally local and accidental in a civilised society. Moreover, the institutions under discussion here are not only very widespread practices which one could claim are naturally invented by men in identical circumstances; they are not only important myths like that of the Flood, rites like that of sacrifice, domestic organisations like the maternal family, juristic practices like blood vengeance – they are also very complex legends or superstitions, thoroughly particular customs, and practices as strange as the *couvade* or the *levirate*. Once these similarities have been established, it becomes inadmissible to explain comparable phenomena by causes which are particular to one society and one era; the human mind refuses to accept regularity and similarity as fortuitous.

It is true that although history does not show the reasons why analogous institutions exist in related civilisations, it sometimes claims to explain the facts by chronologically linking them with one another, while describing in detail the circumstances in which some historic event occurred. However, these relations of pure succession contain nothing that is necessary or intelligible. For the way in which historians assign to an event some other event which they label its 'cause', is entirely arbitrary and not methodical at all. Indeed, inductive procedures are not applicable except where a comparison is easy. As soon as they claim to explain one unique fact by another unique fact, when they refuse to admit that there are necessary and constant links between the facts, historians can perceive causes only through immediate intuition – an operation which escapes from all rule-governed logic as well as from every possibility of verification. It follows from this that historical explanation, impotent to explain observed similarities, is likewise unable to explain a particular event. It presents to human understanding only unintelligible phenomena, unintelligible because they are conceived of as singular, accidental and arbitrarily linked.

A properly sociological explanation, as it has to be conceived if our proposed definition of social phenomenon is accepted, is something quite different. First of all, it does not limit its task to the achievement of the most general aspects of social life. Among social facts it is inappropiate that there is no room to make distinctions according to their greater or lesser generality. The most general is every bit as natural as the most particular; both are equally explicable. Also, all facts exhibiting the characteristics of the social fact as described above can and should be subjects of research. There exist data which the sociologist cannot at present integrate into a system, but there is nothing which he has any a priori right to put outside science and therefore beyond explanation. Thus understood, sociology is not a general and remote view of collective reality, but rather an analysis, as profound and as complete as is possible. It is obliged to study details with a concern for exactness as great as that of the historian. There is no fact, however trivial it may be, that may be neglected as devoid of scientific interest. Even now, one can cite data which seem of absolutely minimal importance and which are nonetheless symptomatic of essential social states that they can help one understand. For example, the order of succession is intimately related to the very constitution of the family, and not only is it not an accidental fact that the distribution is made *per stirpes* or *per capita*, but these two forms of distribution also correspond to very different types of family. Likewise, the penitentiary regime of a society is extremely interesting to the student of society's attitude regarding punishment.

Moreover, whereas historians describe the facts without really explaining them, sociology would undertake to provide an explanation which reason will find satisfactory. It seeks to find among the facts, not mere relationships of succession, but intelligible relationships. It wishes to show how social phenomena are produced and what are the forces from which they result. So it must explain the particular facts by the causes that determine them, close and immediate, causes that are capable of producing them. Therefore, sociologists cannot be content, as some are, with indicating very general and remote causes, ones that in any case are not sufficient and are without direct relationship with the facts. Inasmuch as social facts are specific, they can only be explained by causes of the same nature as themselves. Sociological explanation proceeds, therefore, by going from one social phenomenon to another, establishing relationships *only* between social phenomena. Thus sociology will show us how institutions engender one another; for example, how the ancestor cult developed on the basis of death rituals. In cases, it will perceive true coalescences of social phenomena. For example, the widespread notion of sacrifice of a God is explained by a sort of fusion which has taken place between certain sacrificial rites and certain mythical notions. Sometimes the facts of social structure are interlinked one with another; for example, the formation of towns can be linked to more or less extensive migrations from villages to towns, from rural districts to industrial districts, also to movements of colonisation, to the state of communications, etc. In other cases the structure of a particular type of society will explain certain specific institutions, for example, the arrangement in towns produces certain forms of property, cult, etc.

But how do social facts thus produce one another? When we say that institutions produce other institutions by means of development, coalescence etc., we do not conceive of them as some sort of autonomous realities capable by themselves of having a mysterious efficacy of a particular kind. Likewise, when we connect such and such a social practice to the form of groups, we do not consider it possible that the geographic distribution of individuals affects social life directly and without an intermediary. Institutions exist only in the representations of them made by society. All their living force comes from the sentiments of which they are the objects; if they are strong and respected, it is because these sentiments are lively; if they give way, it is because these institutions have lost all authority in the minds of the population. Likewise, if changes in social structure act upon institutions, it is because they modify the state of the ideas and the tendencies pertaining to the institution; for example, if the formation of the city strongly accentuates the regime of the patriarchal family, it is because the complex of ideas and sentiments that constitute the life of the family change necessarily in proportion as the city grows in density. To employ current language, one could say that all the force of social facts comes to them from attitudes.[3] Attitudes are what dictate moral rules and sanction them, directly or indirectly. Indeed, one can even say that all change in institutions is basically a change in attitudes. Because the collective sentiments of pity for the criminal enter into a struggle with the collective sentiments calling for punishment, the penal regime grows progressively milder. Everything occurs in the sphere of public opinion, but this latter is precisely what we call the system of collective representations. Social facts are therefore causes because they are representations or act on representations. At the inner foundation of social life stands a whole group of representations.

In the foregoing sense, then, sociology could be said to be a psychology. We could accept this formulation, but on the express condition of adding that this psychology is specifically distinct from individual psychology. The representations which are handled by the former are very different in their nature from the representations dealt with by the latter. This has already emerged from what we have said with reference to the characteristics of the social phenomenon, for it is evident that facts possessing such very different properties cannot belong to a single species. There exist, in conscious minds, collective representations which are distinct from individual representations. Of course, societies are made up only of individuals and, consequently, collective representations are only due to the manner in which the individuals can act and react upon each other within a constituted group.[4] These actions and reactions, however, generate psychic phenomena of a new type that are capable of evolving by themselves, of mutually modifying one another, and whose grouping forms a definite system. Not only are collective representations made up of other elements than individual representations, but furthermore they have in reality another object. What they express is the very state of the society. While the facts of the individual consciousness always express in a more or less remote fashion a state of the organism, collective representations always express in some degree a state of the social group. They translate (or, to employ philosophical language, they 'symbolise') its actual structure, the manner in which it reacts in the face of some particular event, the sentiment which it has of itself or of its own interests. The psychic life of society is, therefore, constituted from quite different material from that of the individual.

This is not to say, however, that there could be between them a break in continuity. No doubt, the psyches from which society is formed are combined there in new forms, resulting in new realities. Nevertheless, one can pass from facts of individuals to collective representations by a continuous series of transitions. One easily perceives some of these intermediaries: from the individual one passes insensibly to society, for example, when one arranges in a series the facts of epidemic imitation, the movements of crowds, collective hallucination, etc. Conversely the social becomes individual. It exists only in the individual, but each individual has only a particle of it. And yet this impression of social things on the individual is altered by the particular state of the consciousness which receives them. Everyone speaks his mother tongue in his own fashion, and each author in the end establishes his own preferred syntax and vocabulary. In the same way, each individual makes his own morality, has his individual system of morals. Similarly, each prays and worships according to his own leanings. But these facts are not explicable if one appeals only to individual phenomena in order to comprehend them; they become explicable, however, when one starts from social facts. To demonstrate this, let us take a precise case of individual religion, that of individual totemism. First, from a certain point of view, these facts remain still social and constitute institutions.

It is an article of faith in certain tribes that each individual has his own totem; likewise at Rome, each citisen had his *genius*; in Catholicism each of the faithful has a patron saint. However, there is more. These phenomena stem simply from the fact that a social institution is refracted and disfigured in individuals. If, in addition to his clan totem, each warrior has his individual totem – if one is believed to be related to lizards, whereas another feels himself linked with ravens – it is because each individual has constituted his own totem on the pattern of the clan totem.

It will now be clear what we understand by the phrase collective representations and in what sense we can say that social phenomena can be phenomena of consciousness, without being also phenomena of the individual consciousness. We have also seen what kinds of relations exist between social phenomena.

We are now in a position to state more precisely the formula of sociological explanation that we proffered earlier, when we said that it goes from one social phenomenon to another social phenomenon. From the foregoing, the reader will have glimpsed the existence of two major orders of social phenomena: the facts of social structure, that is, the forms of the group, the manner in which the elements are arranged therein; and the collective representations in which institutions are set out. With that stated, we can say that all sociological explanation falls under one of the three following categories: either (1) it links one collective representation with another collective representation, for example, penal compensation for private vengeance; or (2) it links a collective representation to a fact of social structure as its cause; thus the formation of towns is seen as the cause of the formation of an urban law, the origin of a major part of our system of property; or (3) it links facts of social structure to the collective representations which have determined them; thus certain mythical notions have dominated migratory movements of the Hebrews and the Islamic Arabs; the fascination exercised by great cities is a cause of emigration by rural people.

Admittedly, it may seem that such explanations are circular, since the forms of the group are presented sometimes as effects and sometimes as causes of collective representations. This real circularity, however, does not involve any *petitio principii* or begging of the question: it is a feature of things themselves. Nothing is so pointless as to ask whether ideas have created societies or whether societies, once formed, have given birth to collective ideas. These are inseparable phenomena, between which there is no scope for establishing either a logical or a chronological priority.

Viewed in these terms, sociological explanation does not in any degree merit the reproach of being materialist that has sometimes been made. In the first place, it is independent of all metaphysics, materialist or otherwise. Moreover, in fact, it assigns a preponderant role to the psychic element of social life – beliefs and collective sentiments. From another side, however, it escapes the defects of ideology. For collective representations should not be conceived of as developing by themselves, by virtue of a kind of internal dialectic that forces them to become increasingly refined, so as to approach the ideal of rationality. If the family or criminal law have changed, this is not a consequence of the rational progress of thought which, step by step, has spontaneously rectified its primitive errors. The attitudes and sentiments of the collectivity change only if the social states on which they depend have changed correspondingly. Thus, to explain some social transformation, for example, the transition from polytheism to monotheism, it is no good pointing out that it constitutes progress, that it is more true or more moral, because the question is precisely what it is that has determined the religion to become truer or more moral in this way, in other words, to become what it has in fact become. Social phenomena are no more self-moving than the other phenomena of nature. The cause of a social fact must always be sought outside of that fact. This is to say that the sociologist's goal is not to discover some law of progress or of general evolution which has dominated the past and will predetermine the future. There is no unique universal law of social phenomena. There is a multitude of laws of varying degrees of generality. To explain, in sociology as in all science, is thus to discover more or less fragmentary laws, that is, to link definite facts in terms of definite relations.

II. The Method of Sociology

Essays on method in sociology abound in sociological literature. As a general rule, they mingle with all kinds of philosophical considerations on society, the State, etc. The first works to study the method of sociology in an appropriate manner were those of Comte and John Stuart Mill. Despite their importance, however, these two philosophers' methodological observations still retained an extreme generality, like the science which they intended to found. Recently, Durkheim has attempted to define more precisely the manner in which sociology should proceed in approaching the study of particular facts.

There can, of course, be no question of formulating the rules of sociological method completely and definitively. For a method is only to be distinguished abstractly from the science itself. It is only articulated and organised gradually as the science advances. We propose merely to analyse a certain number of scientific procedures already sanctioned by usage.

Definition

Like all science, sociology should begin the study of each problem with a definition. It is essential above everything else to indicate and to limit the field of the research in order to know what one is talking about. These definitions are preliminary, and consequently provisional. They cannot and should not express the essence of the phenomena to be studied, but simply designate them clearly and distinctly. Nevertheless, no matter how external they may be, they remain indispensable, for without definitions, every science is exposed to confusions and errors. Without them, a sociologist will give different meanings to a single word in the course of a single work, and as a result, will commit grave mistakes. For example, concerning the theory of the family, many authors indiscriminately employ the terms, tribe, village and clan, to designate one and the same thing. Moreover, without definitions, mutual understanding among scholars becomes impossible – discussion occurs with everybody talking at cross-purposes. A good many of the debates triggered by the theory of the family and marriage stem from the absence of definitions – thus some writers label as 'monogamy' what others do not designate by that term; some confuse the legal regime requiring monogamy with simple de facto monogamy, contrasting with others who distinguish these two orders of facts, which are in reality very different.

Naturally definitions of this kind are constructed. Under them one assembles and designates a collection of facts wherein one perceives a fundamental similarity. They are not, however, constructed a priori; they are the résumé of an initial work, an initial rapid review of the facts, of which the common characteristics stand out. Their particular purpose is to substitute an initial scientific notion in place of commonsense notions. Above all, it is essential to disengage from current prejudices that are more dangerous in sociology than in any other science. It is not advisable to adopt without scrutiny a customary classification as if it were a scientific definition. Plenty of ideas still in common use in many social sciences do not appear to be any more grounded in reason than they are grounded in fact and should be banished from a rational terminology. For example, the notions of paganism and even fetishism do not correspond to anything real. In other contexts, serious research leads to the reuniting of what the multitude split up, or discriminating what the multitude conflate together. For example, the science of religions has combined the taboos of impurity and those of purity in a single genus, because they are both taboos; conversely, it has carefully distinguished death rituals from ancestor cults.

These definitions become more exact and more positive the greater one's endeavour is to designate things by their objective characteristics. By 'objective characteristics' we mean those characteristics which such and such a social phenomenon has in itself, that is, those which do not depend upon our sentiments or our personal opinions. Thus we should not define the rite of sacrifice in terms of our more or less rational idea, but rather by the external characteristics which it displays as a social and religious fact, external to and independent of us. Conceived of in this fashion, definition becomes an important step in any research. Even though external, these characteristics which define the social phenomenon to be studied correspond nonetheless to essential characteristics which will be revealed by the analysis. In addition, well-constructed definitions can put the researcher on the path to important discoveries. When crime is defined as an act that infringes in a hostile manner on the rights of individuals, the only crimes are the acts so regarded at present: homicide, theft, etc. When crime is defined as an act which provokes an organised reaction from the collectivity, however, one is led to include under the definition all the truly primitive forms of crime, in particular the violations of religious rules, for example, the rules about taboo.

Lastly, these preliminary definitions constitute a scientific guarantee of the very first rank. Once they have been stated, they obligate and limit the sociologist. They clarify all his operations, they permit effective criticism and discussion. For, thanks to them, an entire pattern of well-designated facts imposes itself upon the student, and explanation must take all of them into account. In this way one avoids all the capricious arguments where the author passes as he pleases from one subject to another, and borrows his evidence from the most heterogeneous categories of facts. Furthermore, one avoids a fault that is still committed by some of the best works in sociology, for example, Frazer's book on totemism. This fault consists in collecting only the facts favourable to one's thesis and not searching sufficiently for contrary facts. In general, people do not take enough trouble to integrate all the facts into one theory; one assembles only those which can be superimposed exactly. Thus, with initial good definitions, all the social facts of a single order are presented and impose themselves on the observer, and one is obliged to explain not only concordances but also differences.

Observation of the Facts

As we have already seen, definition assumes an initial review of the facts, a sort of tentative observation. We must now speak of methodical observation, that is, observation which establishes each of the stated facts. Observation of social phenomena is not, as one might have thought at first glance, a pure narrative procedure. Sociology should do more than describe the facts; it must, in reality, constitute them. First, more so in sociology than in any other science, there exist no brute facts that one could, as it were, photograph. All scientific observation bears upon phenomena methodically chosen and isolated from others, that is, abstracted. Even more than any others, social phenomena cannot be studied all at once in all of their details and all of their relations. They are too complex and one must proceed by abstractions and by successive divisions of the difficulties. While it abstracts the facts, however, sociological observation is nonetheless scrupulous and careful to establish them exactly. Social facts are very difficult to attain, to disentangle from the documents. An even more delicate task is to analyse them, and, in some cases, to give approximate quantifications. What is needed, then, are special and rigorous procedures of observation; employing the usual language, the need is for critical methods. The use of these methods naturally varies according to the varied phenomena observed by sociologists. This is why there exist different means for analyzing a religious rite and for describing the formation of a town. Despite this fact, the spirit and the method of the work remain identical, and critical methods can only be classified in terms of the nature of the documents to which they are applied: some are statistical documents, nearly always modern and recent, others are historical documents. The numerous problems presented by the utilisation of these documents are somewhat different, but at the same time they are somewhat analogous.

In all work based upon statistical elements, it is important, even indispensable, to expound carefully the way in which one has arrived at the data which have been employed. In the current state of the various judicial, economic, demographic and other statistics, each document invites the most severe critique. Consider, for example, official documents, which in general offer the most guarantees of reliability. The documents themselves must be examined in all their details, and it is important to know the principles which have guided their production. In the absence of meticulous precautions, one risks ending up with false data. For example, it is impossible to use the statistical information on suicide in England, since in order to evade the rigours of the law, most suicides in that country are reported under the rubric of death following insanity; thus the statistics are vitiated in their very foundations. In addition, it is necessary to carefully reduce to comparability the data available from diverse sources. Having failed to proceed in this fashion, many studies in the sociology of morals contain serious errors. Comparisons have been made between figures that do not at all have the same meaning in the various European statistical series. In fact, the statistics are based on the codes, and the various legal codes have neither the same classifications nor even the same nomenclature. For example, English law does not distinguish negligent homicides from wilful homicides. Furthermore, like all scientific observation, statistical observation should tend to be as exact and as detailed as possible. Often, in fact, the characteristic of the facts changes, when a general observation is replaced by an increasingly precise analysis. Thus, a map drawn up of suicides in France by *arrondissements* makes one notice different phenomena shown on a map drawn up by *départements*.

So far as historical and ethnographic documents are concerned sociology should adopt roughly the procedures of 'historical criticism'. Sociology cannot make use of concocted data and must therefore establish the truth of the information that it uses. These procedures of criticism are a technique all the more necessary in that, not without reason, sociologists have often been reproached for neglecting them. For example, the accounts of travellers and ethnographers have been used without sufficient discrimination. Knowledge of the sources, and a severe critique of them, would have allowed sociologists to establish an unchallengeable basis for their theories concerning the elementary forms of social life. One may, moreover, hope that the progress of history and of ethnography will increasingly facilitate the work by supplying unchallengeable information. The sociologist has everything to hope for from progress in these two disciplines, but even though the sociologist may have the same critical requirements as the historian, he must conduct his critique following different principles because he studies the facts in another spirit and with a view to a different goal. First, so far as possible, he observes only social facts, the basic facts; and we know how recent concerns of this kind are in the historical sciences, where, for example, we do not have many good histories of the economic organisation even of our own country. Next, sociology does not study the facts by asking insoluble questions whose solution, in any case, has only minimal explanatory value. Thus, in the absence of definite monuments, it is not indispensable to state a precise date for the Rig-Veda: this is impossible, and basically does not matter. The date of some social fact, for example, a prayer ritual, need not be known in order for the facts to be useful in sociology, provided that its antecedents, its concomitants, its consequences – in a word, the entire social framework surrounding it – are known. Finally, the sociologist does not research exclusively the singular details of each phenomenon. Having concentrated particularly on the biographies of great men and of tyrants, historians are now above all concerned with 'collective biography'. They concern themselves with the particular nuances of the mores and the beliefs of each group, large or small. They seek for what separates, what singularises, and tend to depict what one might call the ineffable element in each civilisation. For example, the general belief is that the study of the Vedic religion is reserved for Sanskritists. The sociologist, in contrast, concerns himself to discover in social facts what is general at the same time as what is characteristic. For him, a well-conducted observation should give a definite outcome, a sufficiently adequate expression of the observed fact. To make use of an ascertained social fact, integral knowledge of the history, language or civilisation, is not necessary. Relative but precise knowledge of the fact in question will suffice to ensure that it can and must enter into the system that sociology intends to build. The more so, as in numerous cases, it is still indispensable for the sociologist to go back to the original sources, but problem here lies, not in the facts, but with the historians who have not been able to subject them to real analysis. Sociology requires secure and impersonal observations, utilisable by whomever studies facts of the same order. The details and the contexts of all the facts are infinite, and no one could ever exhaust them. Pure history will never stop describing, expressing subtle nuances, and particularising circumstances. In contrast, a sociological observation made with care, a phenomenon well studied and analysed in its integrity, loses almost all dating, quite like a doctor's observation, or an extraordinary experiment in a laboratory. Scientifically described, the social fact becomes an element of science, and ceases to belong

especially to a particular country or a particular period. The force of scientific observation has, so to speak, placed it beyond time and space.

Physics ?
Economics

Systematisation of the Facts

Like any science sociology does not speculate on pure ideas and does not limit itself to registering facts. It aims to give them a rational system, seeking to determine their relations in a manner that renders them intelligible. It remains for us to state by what procedures these relations can be ascertained. Occasionally – actually rather rarely – the relations will be found, so to speak, already established. In fact, in sociology, as in all science, there exist some phenomena so typical that one need only to analyse them well to discover immediately certain unsuspected relationships. Fison and Howitt encountered a phenomenon of this kind when they threw new light on the primitive forms of the family by explaining the system of kinship and exogamic classes in certain Australian tribes. As a general rule, however, we do not reach these crucial facts directly by simple observation. So an entire range of special methodological procedures must be employed to establish the relations which exist between facts. On this point, sociology has a status of inferiority compared with other sciences. Experimentation is not possible; one cannot voluntarily create typical social facts which could then be studied. It is therefore necessary to resort to the comparison of diverse social facts of a single category in different societies, so as to try and isolate their essence. Basically, a well-managed comparison in sociology can yield results equivalent to those of experimentation. One proceeds very much like the zoologists, notably like Darwin. With one single exception, the latter could not conduct true experiments and create various species; he had to make a general tabulation of the facts he knew about the origin of species and from the methodical comparison of these facts he derived his hypotheses. Likewise in sociology, Morgan, having ascertained the identity of the Iroquois, Hawaiian, and Fijian familial systems, could hypothesise clans based on maternal descent. Moreover, in general, when comparison has been undertaken by genuine savants, it has always given good results in the matter of social facts. Even when it has led to a theoretical conclusion, as in the works of the English school of anthropology, it did at least end by developing a general classification of an enormous number of facts.

Moreover, scholars are trying and should try to render comparison ever more exact. Certain authors, Tylor and Steinmetz among others, have even proposed and employed a statistical method, the first with reference to marriage, the second with reference to punishment and to endocannibalism. They expressed numerically the concordances and the differences between the ascertained facts. The results of this method, however, are far from satisfactory, because they have collected facts drawn from the most diverse and the most heterogeneous societies, registered in documents of widely disparate value. They thus attach excessive importance to the number of cases, the accumulated facts. They do not show a sufficient interest in the quality of their cases or in their reliability, in the demonstrative value of the facts, or in their comparability. It is probably preferable to renounce all such pretensions to exactness, and it would be better to limit oneself to elementary but rigorous comparisons. In the first place, it is important to compare only facts of the same order, that is, those that fit within the definition stated at the beginning of the work. Thus the researcher would do well, in a theory of the family a propos of the clan, to assemble only facts about the clan and not to combine them with ethnographic information which in reality concerns the tribe and the local group, often confused with the clan. Secondly, it is necessary to arrange the facts thus compared in carefully constituted series. In other words, one arranges the different forms in which the facts are presented following some particular order, either an order of increasing or decreasing complexity, or some other kind of variation. For example, in a theory of the patriarchal family, one will rank the Hebraic family below the Greek family, and the latter below the Roman family. Thirdly, alongside this series, one has other series available, constructed in the same fashion, composed of other social facts. And from the relationships that one grasps between these diverse series, one sees the hypotheses emerge. For example, it is possible to link the evolution of the patriarchal family to the evolution of the city: from the Hebrews to the Greeks, from these to the Romans. In Roman law itself, the power of the paterfamilias is seen to increase in proportion to the extent that the city knits itself together more closely.

The Scientific Character of Sociological Hypotheses

Thus one arrives at the devising of hypotheses and their verification with the aid of well-observed facts, for a well-defined problem. Naturally, these hypotheses are not inevitably sound; a good number of those that appear obvious to us today will some day be abandoned. But while they may not possess the quality of absolute truth, they exhibit all the characteristics of scientific hypotheses. First, they are truly explanatory; they state the 'why' and the 'how' of things. A legal rule such as the rule of civil responsibility is not explained by referring to the classic 'will of the legislator,' or by some general 'virtues' of human nature which have rationally created this institution. The rule is explained by the whole evolution of the system of responsibility. Second, they have, indeed, the character of necessity and therefore of generality which is that of methodical induction and which can, in some cases perhaps, allow prediction. For example, one could almost state as a law that ritual practices tend to become rarified and spiritualised in the course of development of the universalist religions. Third, and in our view this is the most important point, such hypotheses are eminently criticisable and verifiable. In a true work of sociology, each of the points treated can be criticised. Such works are remote from that impalpable froth of facts or those phantasmagorias of ideas and words that the public often take for sociology, but in which there are neither precise ideas, nor rational system, nor the close study of facts. The hypothesis becomes an element of precise discussion; one can dispute, correct the method, the initial definition, the facts invoked, the comparisons established, in such a way that progress is possible for the science.

At this point, it is necessary to forestall an objection. Critics may be tempted to say that, before establishing itself, sociology should complete a total inventory of all social facts. Thus they might demand of the theorist of the family that he completely ransack all the ethnographic, historical and statistical documents relative to this question. Tendencies of this kind are to be feared in our science. Timidity in the face of the facts is every bit as dangerous as excessive audacity; the abdications of empiricism are every bit as fatal as hasty generalisations. Firstly, while science does require increasingly complete reviews of the facts, it never demands a total inventory, which in any case is impossible. A biologist is not expected to have observed all the facts of digestion, in the whole range of animals, in order to attempt theories of digestion. The sociologist should do likewise; he, too, does not need in-depth knowledge of all the social facts of a particular category in order to fashion a theory about them. He should work step by step. To his provisional but carefully enumerated and specified knowledge, there correspond provisional hypotheses. The generalisations made and the systems proposed are valid for the moment for all the known or unknown facts of the same order as the facts which are explained. One is free to modify the theories as new facts come to be known or as science, which every day becomes more precise, discovers new aspects in previously known facts. Outside these increasingly close approximations to the phenomena, there is room only for dialectic discussions or learned encyclopaedias, both of which lack true utility, because they do not propose any explanation. Moreover, if the work of induction has been done methodically, it is impossible that the results arrived at by the sociologist could be denuded of all reality. The hypotheses express the facts, and consequently they always contain at least a portion of truth. Science may complete them, correct them, or transform them, but it will never fail to utilise them.

III. The Divisions of Sociology

Sociology claims to be a science and to be connected with the established scientific tradition. However, it is none the less free vis-à-vis existing classifications. It can divide up the work otherwise than has been done thus far.

In the first place, sociology considers as its own a certain number of problems which, thus far, have belonged to sciences which are not among the 'social sciences'. It breaks up these sciences, relinquishing to them what is their own proper subject-matter, and retaining for itself all the facts of an exclusively social order. Thus, geography hitherto has dealt with questions of frontiers, networks of communication, social density, etc. Now these are not questions of geography, but questions of sociology, because what are involved are not cosmic phenomena, but phenomena which are directly related to the nature of societies. Similarly, sociology appropriates for itself the results already achieved by criminal anthropology regarding a certain range of phenomena which are not somatic phenomena, but rather social facts.

In the second place, among the sciences which are ordinarily called social sciences, there are some which are not properly referred to as sciences. They exhibit only an artificial unity, and sociology should deconstruct them. Such are statistics and ethnography, both of which are considered as forming distinct sciences, even though all they do, with their respective procedures, is to study highly disparate phenomena that belong in reality to different parts of sociology. Statistics, as we have seen, is simply a method for observing the varied phenomena of modern social life. Today statistics studies demographic, moral and economic phenomena indiscriminately. In our view, there should not be statisticians, but rather sociologists who in order to study moral and economic phenomena, to study groups, prepare moral, economic, demographic and other statistics. Our view is the same respecting ethnography. This has for its sole raison d'être the study of phenomena that occur in the so-called 'savage peoples'. It studies indiscriminately moral, juristic, and religious phenomena, technologies, arts, etc. In contrast, sociology does not naturally distinguish between the institutions of 'savage' peoples and those of 'barbarous' or 'civilised' nations. It incorporates under its definitions the most elementary as well as the most evolved phenomena. And, for example, in a study of family or punishment, it is obliged to consider 'ethnographic' facts as well as 'historical' facts, both kinds alike being social facts and not differing except as regards the way in which they are observed.

On the other hand, sociology adopts and makes its own the great divisions, already observed by the various comparative sciences, of institutions of which sociology claims to be the heir – the sciences of law, religions, political economy, etc. From that point of view, it divides rather easily into special sociologies. In adopting that subdivision, however, it does not slavishly follow the ordinary classifications which for the most part are empirical or practical in origin, as for example, those of the science of law. Above all it does not establish between the facts, those water-tight compartments which ordinarily exist between the various special sciences. The sociologist who studies legal and moral facts in order to understand them must often apply to religious phenomena. The student of property should consider this phenomenon under its double aspect – legal and economic – even though these two sides of a single phenomenon are ordinarily studied by different scholars.

In this way, then, while joining closely with the sciences which have preceded it, and even appropriating their results, sociology transforms their classifications. It will be remarked, moreover, that all of the various social sciences have in late years come progressively closer to sociology; increasingly they are becoming special parts of a single science. There is one qualification, however: as sociology achieves a status of true science, with a conscious method, it profoundly changes the very spirit of research, and can lead to new results. In addition, even though numerous results can be retained, each part of sociology cannot coincide exactly with the various existing social sciences. These latter are being transformed, and the introduction of the sociological method has already changed, and will further change, the manner in which social phenomena are studied. Social phenomena are divided into two major orders. On the one hand, there are groups and their structures. There is thus a special part of sociology which will study groups, the number of individuals composing them, and the varying fashions in which they are distributed in space – this is social morphology. On the other hand, there are social phenomena which occur in these groups – institutions or collective representations. These latter in truth constitute the great functions of social life. Each of these functions – religious, juristic, economic, aesthetic, etc. – should first be studied separately and form the subject-matter of a series of relatively independent researches. From this point of view, there will be a sociology of religion, a sociology of morals, a sociology of law, a sociology of technology, etc. Subsequently, given all of these special studies, it will be possible to constitute the final part of sociology, that is, general sociology, whose aim will be research on what gives unity to all the social phenomena.

Notes

(Added by Nick Allen)

1. Mauss employs the word *fait* (fact). There are occasions, as here, when *fait* is better translated by phenomenon.
2. Fields (*règnes*). Mauss is referring, no doubt, to a hierarchy of sciences as in Comte.
3. Fr. *opinion*
4. Individuals. The French reads *les consciences individuelles*. The English translation of *conscience* is problematic since in French it implies both consciousness as a human attribute and conscience as a moral concept. Some translators prefer to retain the French. Within the context of this translation, it is thought best to omit the word *conscience*, especially when it is used in the plural, as it is here, and employ the word 'individuals'.

References

1. On the history of sociology
   Bouglé, *Les sciences sociales en Allemagne* (1896).
   Durkheim, 'Les sciences morales en Allemagne', *Revue philosophique* (1887).
   Durkheim, 'La sociologie en France au xixe siècle', *Revue bleue* (May, 1900).
   Espinas, *Sociétés animales*, (préface) (1867).

Fouillée, *La Science sociale contemporaine* (1885).
Groppali, 'La sociologie en Amerique', *Annales de l'Inst. Internat. de sociologie* (1900).
Lévy-Bruhl, *La Philosophie d'Auguste Comte* (1900).

2. On sociology in general
Comte, *Cours de philosophie positive* (vols 4–6).
De Greef, *Introduction à la sociologie* (1886–89).
De Greef, *Transformisme social* (1894).
Espinas, op.cit.
Giddings, *Principles of sociology* (1896).
Gumplowicz, *Grundriss der Sociologie* (1885).
Lester Ward, *Dynamic Sociology* (1897).
Lester Ward, *Outlines of Sociology* (1898).
Schäffle. *Bau und Leben des sozialen Körpers* (1875–81).
Small, *An Introduction to the study of society* (1894).
Spencer, *The Study of Sociology* (1873).
Spencer, *Social Statics: Descriptive Sociology* (1874 et seq.).
Spencer, *Principles of Sociology* (1876 et seq.).
Tarde, *Les Lois de 1'imitation* (1890–95).
Tarde, *Logique sociale* (1895).
Tönnies, *Gemeinschaft und Gesellschaft* (1887).

3. Among the principal works of the organicist school are
Demoor, Massart and Vandervelde, *Evolution régressive en biologie et en sociologie* (1897).
Massart and Vandervelde, *Parasitisme organique et parasitisme social.*
Novikow, *La lutte entre les sociétés humaines* (1893).
Novikow, *Conscience et volonté sociales* (1896).
Worms, *Organisme et société* (1896).

4. The principal periodicals devoted to sociology strictly speaking are the following
American Journal of Sociology
Annales de l'Institut international de sociologie
Année sociologique
Revue internationale de sociologie
Rivista Italiana di sociologia
Zeitschrift fur Sozialwissenschaft

5. On the method of sociology
Comte, op.cit.
Durkheim, *Règles de la méthode sociologique* (1895).
J.S. Mill, *Logic*, Book VI
On selected points see: Bosco, *La Statistica civile e penale* (1898); Langlois and Seignobos, *Introduction aux études historiques* (1898); Tylor, 'On a method of investigating the development of institutions', *Journal of the Anthropological institute*, XVIII, 1889; Steinmetz, *Studien zur ersten Entwickelung der Strafe* (1895–1896); Steinmetz, 'Classification des types sociaux', *Année sociologique* (1900).

Marcel Mauss

SOCIOLOGY:
ITS DIVISIONS AND
THEIR RELATIVE
WEIGHTINGS

First published in French in 1927 as 'Divisions et proportions des divisions de la sociologie', *L'Année sociologique*, n.s. II, pp. 98–176.

Introduction

The plan of the New Series of the *Année sociologique* remains the same as that of the preceding series. We have altered nothing in the framework which Durkheim had slowly elaborated. We follow the established sequence; the materials continue to be distributed among the six accustomed headings: general sociology, sociology of religion, law and morality, economic sociology, and social morphology, and among the three sciences which we group unsatisfactorily under the heading of 'miscellaneous': technology, aesthetics, and linguistics.

Let us be frank. In support of this arrangement, we invoke only two reasons of expediency. On the one hand, we wish to continue a respectable tradition and not upset old and loyal readers of the *Année sociologique*. On the other hand, if we remain confined in the established divisions of the *Année*, it is because we cannot really modify them straight away. None of us as individuals are yet detached, none of us yet know how to detach ourselves from the old disciplines – law, history of religions, political economy – from which our specialities have derived. Moreover, as a group, we are not ready for an effort at renovation which, perhaps, is not yet necessary and which is certainly too great for the surviving handful of Durkheim's disciples. In fact we lack purely sociological specialists in social morphology, linguistics, technology, and aesthetics; their participation would have changed both the aspect of our studies and – a relatively secondary point – even the proportions of the parts of the *Année sociologique*. Finally, all of us having too much to do in our own domains, we lack the time that would be required, and we have not the courage to break with what we know to be merely one fashion in our science, one period in its development, rather than its basis and its truth.

This is a necessary acknowledgement. Surely, if war and sickness had not snatched away from us both our master together with our most valued collaborators, and the best years of our lives; if Durkheim had continued to 'do' the *Année*, he would have come to give it more exact forms and more harmonious proportions. A quarter-century after the foundation of the *Année*, he would have revised this division; he would have matched it to its gradual progress, or at least he would have spurred it on in the direction of what it tended to be. At the very least, he would have attempted to give it a better sequence, and better proportions for each part. Above all else he would, I believe, have at least indicated a division of the facts other than the one which he had adopted and enriched, but about which, as we shall see, he always maintained a certain reserve. Even if he had not been able to revise the sequence he had adopted, he would not have failed to point out the sequence which he thought would one day have to be adopted.

He would thus have called to the reform of our studies a generation of workers not only more numerous, but above all more naturally detached from ancient prejudices, which, by virtue of their youth, they would have forgotten. The younger workers would have distanced themselves from the parent disciplines on which it was necessary to impose, or superpose, or oppose the sociological consideration of facts which they had already studied. Naturally liberated, this new group of workers would, perhaps, under the direction of their elders, have reached the goal.

In any case, and above all scrupulous vis-à-vis facts and recognising the truth, Durkheim would have acknowledged these inevitable facts to which we are resigned as he was resigned. At the beginning of this new phase of the *Année sociologique*, it is necessary that we carefully indicate the limitations that we see on the results acquired by our own work. The confession of ignorance is the scholar's first duty. We do not have the last word, perhaps not even the latest in date; to foster any such illusion in our readers would be extremely dangerous. Playing that game, we could easily lose the authority which we hold from Durkheim. We may, therefore, criticise ourselves and say that the number, the sequence and the proportions of the divisions of sociology as we present them here do not correspond to reality or to the facts, but rather to the present state of our sciences and also to the state of our personal knowledge. Even these divisions into compartments and the principles underlying these divisions must themselves be scrutinised.

Chapter 1

The Sequence or Order
of the Parts of Sociology

The sequence that we continue to follow presents two major disadvantages: neither *general sociology* nor *social morphology* are in their proper position.

Social morphology unites several sciences which are ordinarily separated; but they are improperly separated, poorly defined and, when they are joined, they are even more poorly interrelated, e.g., demography and anthropogeography (cf. Durkheim, reviewing F. Ratzel, *Anthropogéographie*, in the *Année sociologique*, III, 550–58 (1898–99)). We should articulate it better, particularly so far as concerns demography, that statistical lumber room which must be better demarcated, on the one hand from moral statistics, and on the other hand, from the study of the various groups and social organisations (occupations, classes, etc.). In any case, the entire ensemble of morphological studies should be more clearly separated from the others. Morphology is a part, almost a primordial half, and one of the most independent parts of sociology. In particular it should be demarcated from all physiological study, even if it is not distinguished from the other parts of sociology. Morphological phenomena have an extraordinarily conspicuous material aspect, being countable and representable graphically (by maps and diagrams). They are mutually dependent to such a degree that they seem to form a separate domain within the wider social domain. In our opinion, therefore, morphological theory should be either the last or the first of our substantive headings. The first, if one considers that each society's physical body as this appears in time and space (the number of its individuals, the change and stability of the population and its generations, spatial mobility, limits on availability of land, geographic conditions and adaptation to the terrain) should from this point of view be the first object of our studies, whether special or general. Alternatively, if one studies the geographic and demographic distribution of the different social organisations, e.g., temples or occupations within the society, it should come in the last place. In either case, it is badly placed where it is now located in the *Année sociologique*, following the three special sociologies (religious, legal and economic) and preceding the disciplines which we classify together with it under the general and meaningless rubric of 'miscellaneous'. These latter, the sociology of technology, aesthetics, and linguistics, are, like the first three, equally sciences not of the group in its materiality, but of its practices and its representations. In a word, they form part of social physiology or psychology. We place *morphology* at the head of 'miscellaneous' to give it a place of honour, but this location is inappropriate. We shall return to its proportions and, yet once again, to this question of sequence.

As for *general sociology*, the problem is more complicated. This section should be divided into two parts. One part – the history of ideas, methodology, general theory – could remain at the head of the *Année*. In effect, this part pertains to ideas that introduce people to sociology. This section could be entitled 'Preliminaries', since they are matters of the gateway and not of the arcane mysteries within. In contrast, however, another entire part should be presented separately, carefully distinguished from all the rest, at the end of the *Année* and its various sections. This part is concerned, not with one or another order of social phenomena, but with social phenomena in their entirety. Four headings compose it; moreover, these have seen such a development in recent years, and have made such obvious advances – advances in terms of the number of ascertained facts and the quality of the theories that group them – that to remain at the point where we now are will surely be impossible.

In the first place, there has been progress in the study of systems of social facts, of those systems of social facts which surpass the ambit of particular societies and extend to areas and families of societies – in a word, the phenomena so inadequately grouped under the name of *civilisation*. Numerous works are said to be inspired by 'ethnology', by the method of 'cultural history', by that of the 'civilisational morphology', by those of the 'civilisational areas'. As a consequence, the question of the relations that link sociological consideration of social facts is posed in terms very different from those formerly used, and it requires elucidation. All these studies by ethnographers and historians are neither independent of, nor indifferent to, our studies. In principle, they have become feasible and have obviously made progress only alongside the progress of other studies of social facts. In fact, the principal types of legal, economic and religious institutions, the principal types of implements, industries and the fine arts had to be determined, before the geographic extension and the historic filiation of these types could be studied. It is only this determination of *genre* that allows one to sense the particularities of each institution, each technique, etc., and by making us sense these particularities, allows the historical relations to emerge. Without this support from sociological theory, history – frequently impossible in these matters – could not distinguish between the societies that are supposed to have had contacts with each other. Moreover, these contacts and these filiations can only be conceived when the principal families of languages and the principal races have been delimited.

Inversely, a better historical description of civilisational relations between various societies will necessarily affect our studies from many points of view. On the one hand, it will eliminate a number of these grievous so-called evolutions which supposedly occurred independently in so many societies; on the other hand, however, this elimination will emphasise the necessity of recognising certain other coincidences. Thus the character of certain institutions and modes of representations will no longer appear as simply historical but as natural, as inherent in man's social nature. However, our sociological labours can benefit even from the historical point of view, because social phenomena – institutions, forms of artefacts, fashions of thought, of grouping, and of reproduction, etc. – are finally seen as being intimately linked to each society and its sphere of influence and no longer to pan-human and psychological reasons. The sifting of the historical from the social, the contingent from the accidental, and the chronological from the necessary, the logical and the rational will hereafter be done better. Facts considered from two viewpoints will be better classified. What is truly general will be better separated from the particular. Nevertheless all these phenomena will clearly appear as sociological.

Another series of questions whose importance has greatly increased obviously forms part of sociology – namely, *social systems*. There are grave disadvantages in the fashion in which most of us proceed most of the time. Societies and the phenomena of their life appear as things parcelled out, broken up into institutions, notions, etc., separated, divided, special. The most serious criticisms that the historians have made of our methods concern our fashion of expounding the facts, which is too general and yet insufficiently synthetic for their taste. In the numerous prefaces to the volumes in his splendid collection *L'évolution de l'humanité*, M. Berr, if we understand him correctly, particularly and often repeats this relatively legitimate observation. The criticism applies, however, more to the sociologist's texts than to his fashion of thinking and working. Like any science, sociology has hastened to what is most urgent and easy, and also most useful; it has abstracted before seeking the basic relationships or describing ensembles. Moreover, it has dealt with only a small number of facts, which we have simply labelled, when what was needed was to know them all. But firstly, in a quarter of a century of productive effort, Durkheim never lost sight of the problem of the whole, which is basically that of *The Division of Labour* and of *The Elementary Forms of the Religious Life*; and then Durkheim, Simiand, Hubert and others – we have always had the sense of what there is that is specific to each society. In fact each system of social facts has its essence, its quiddity, whether this sets the limits for such and such a 'savage tribe', or whether it constitutes the individuality, what one calls the soul or the psychology – most inappropriate terms – of a great people. This study of the mutual fit between the various pieces which compose the machinery of a society – its adjustment to its habitat, and its capacity, in these conditions, to create things, to initiate customs, sciences and fine arts, ultimately to develop its final character,– such a study we have always basically proposed as the source and as the final confluence of all our narrower studies. The reader will forgive us for citing as an example of this work the memoir that we published in the *Année* on Eskimo societies in collaboration with the lamented Beuchat, and also with Durkheim. Further, we take the liberty of offering as a model to historians the researches which M. Granet has just published, in the *Travaux* of the *Année*, concerning the civilisation in which imperial China developed. The importance we attach to such books as the splendid *History of the English People* by Elie Halévy is another proof of our good will. Finally, it will become clear in coming years how deeply we are interested in the events which, this time statistically innumerable, characterise the formation of new societies before our very eyes. Certainly, all this is only tentative. Numerous facts must here be classified in the light of numerous theories. At the moment it is sufficient for us to indicate the position where ideally we should locate these studies: at the end of 'general sociology', rather than letting them be unfortunately parcelled out, fragmented, and arbitrarily distributed among several headings, especially 'legal systems' and 'general sociology'.

The production of recent years has been directed towards a third problem, whose philosophical interest has rendered it popular. Thanks to us, it is at present fashionable to interrogate sociology on the *origins of reason*, the primitive forms of thought, etc. Scholars have abstained, wrongly in our opinion, from studying evolved or semi-learned forms. In the *Année*, these problems are unsatisfactorily divided between 'general sociology' and 'religious sociology'. Thanks to M. Meillet, we touch on these problems also under 'linguistic sociology'; we shall have to return to this point later. However, to repeat the point, we know that they really belong to that general sociology whose basic outlines Durkheim formulated quite early. However, instead of forming part of the prolegomena, they form the conclusions of our sciences and not merely of some of them, but of the whole set. In this domain, partial considerations are infinitely dangerous. The notion of class or *genre* is mainly juristic in origin, as Durkheim and I have assumed; as Hubert has said, the notion of time, and as Durkheim wrote in the *Elementary Forms of the Religious Life*, the notion of soul and, in some pages of the same book which have been too little noticed, the notion of the Whole are mainly religious or symbolic in origin – none of these arguments mean to say that every other general notion has had the same kind of origin. We do not at all believe that. There remain to be studied many other categories, both living and dead, deriving from many other origins, and in particular categories of a technical nature. To cite only the mathematical concepts of Number and Space, who will ever say enough and with sufficient exactitude the part which weaving, basket-making, carpentry, nautical art, the wheel and the potter's wheel have had in the origins of geometry, arithmetic, and mechanics? We shall never tire of recalling the splendid observations by Frank Cushing, profound observer and inspired sociologist, on 'manual concepts' (*Amer. Anthrop.*, vol. 5 (1892); cf. *Année*, Vol. II). We would never come to an end of listing the various activities and also the various ideas whose *forms* are at bottom general ideas, including those which are still at bottom our own ideas. These studies of the forms of thought, primitive or not, should appear at the end, to crown and to synthesise our studies.

In this last place in general sociology, one should find a fourth group of researches: those on *politics* or *theory of the state*, and also, occasionally, those on the applications of politics and of morality, which we shall discuss later. We still divide them rather badly; in part they come at the head of the *Année*, with general sociology, and in part we assign them either to sociology of law or to economic sociology. This division, however, does not take into account one of the great discoveries of modern times, imposed by the evidence and by facts which are often cruel. In reality, an important part of our political and social life is not political, but technological or economic, depending upon what predominates: whether it is the problem of industrial equipment or production in terms of sales. In addition, even this consideration (almost exclusive in certain schools) of what are confused under the label of 'economic phenomena' is still erroneous because the facts are demographic or technological as well. F. Simiand has frequently shown this with reference to economic phenomena properly so-called. What explains a social fact is not one or another order of facts, but rather the total ensemble of facts. For example, the recruitment of a workforce, the location of an industry and the conquest of a market require the practical man, the merchant, the manufacturer, the financier and the scientist, i.e., many other things and many other individuals besides the workers. They also require more than shares of stock or machines: an area of land, someone's property in some particular region; and, most important, a body of men already trained in some particular occupation or capable of being trained; another group for the sale of products; needs which are to be satisfied or to be stimulated; and adequate monetary resources. All these basic factors are no longer simply economic; some are morphological, the others are 'psychological', as one says – most inappropriately – meaning thereby that they stem from a traditional order, institutional or ideal, or simply from public opinion, like fashion. Fundamentally, all political studies, all practical conclusions drawn by our sciences, all doctrines of conservatism, like all projects of reform, reorganisation, and social revolution, all *ex post facto* justifications of situations that have already arisen, all the descriptions of future society and even the dreams which are so much – indeed, too much – in vogue in our times, relate at every moment to the totality of the social body, even when they claim to consider only a single organ in that body; precisely as in the majority of cases, the internal remedy administered by the doctor acts not only on the part of the body which he intends to heal, but on the entire individual. This is why, in our opinion – and even though in some cases one or another part of social science can occasionally indicate some practical solutions to a problem which they pose – the majority of political researches should be preceded by inquiries going well beyond the domain to which they have been arbitrarily limited.

Let us consider a pair of examples. In France and in America two questions are everywhere the order of the day: the question of social insurance, and the question of immigration or its correlative emigration. In these two cases, legislative bodies themselves and public opinion have appealed to scientific studies and have invited distinguished sociologists to associate themselves with the work. This demonstrates already that sociology serves some purpose and even that it involves general sociology.

Social insurance is said to belong to economic science. It is in fact specialists in the law faculties who discuss the topic in their teaching. But who fails to see that the distinction is purely scholastic and depends only upon the accidents of universities' organisational structures, on current pedantry? In itself, the problem is of a statistical kind, particularly demographic. The number, sex and age of the insured, their death rate, their rates of sickness, their birth rate and their occupational accidents are the essential data. This stands out with great clarity in the book which Ferdinand-Dreyfus has devoted to this question in France. Moreover, the problem is moral, even more than it is political or economic, for it is a principle of social justice, a matter of sentiment – let us say the word – which determines the benefits of the insured, the assessments of the contributors, and apportions both. Sociology is there only in order to refine, clarify and affirm this sentiment, to render it conscious and to bring about its practical satisfaction. Further, as is obvious, it is sociology in its entirety, and not simply the science of economics that is involved here.

In the same fashion, the cooperation of the whole of sociology is required for the study of those serious, contemporary and urgent problems raised in America by immigration and, elsewhere, by emigration. The direction of these various currents, which both can and should be directed and which are in fact directed, depends on a simultaneously complete, exact and delicate study of the society from which people emigrate and of the elements which immigrate. The strength of this dependence is what emerges from the remarkable studies which preceded recent legislation in the United States or which at the moment are working on its effects, particularly those of Miss Edith Abbott. Those dry statistics of origins, like those to which our continental censuses have been limited, are no longer sufficient. There are all sorts of other data, statistical phenomena and non-statistical phenomena, moral, ideal and even material and biological phenomena, which are at this moment enumerated, weighed, divided, balanced and selected. The sociologist should note this victory for our science, this possibly somewhat excessive prestige, this authority that has been somewhat naively conferred upon him in the other continent. For the first time in history, not only the problem of the confection of a race, but the much nobler problem of the formation of a nation and its moral and physical constitution, are posed over there in a conscious fashion and treated in a way which intends to be rational. The question is how to form an American stock and an American society with its traditional moral nature and its capacities of moral, technical and intellectual development, composed of an optimum number of fine and healthy humans. To be sure, not all the arguments thrown about in the debate are from pure science and indeed they are not always scientific or honest. Some prejudices, some a priori assumptions, some sordid interests, electoral or even private, blend themselves in studies having a sound sociological cast; sometimes they conceal themselves beneath these studies; but this hypocrisy is simply homage rendered to the science. Finally, chance also governs events. No matter – the data have been assembled. The Americans have not limited themselves to getting the data registered by official bureaux and offices or by research institutes; the dough of facts has been kneaded with the yeast of rational moral reflection which is still working on them, perhaps more than is widely believed, under the distant influence of French political traditions. It is recognised over there that the problem of Americanisation is a problem of 'civics'. This is indeed how it should be posed. Material and anthropological recruitment, as well as moral, economic, technical and educational recruitment, should be the object not only of knowledge, but also of choice. We see how a great people puts its entire social system, its whole demographic composition, at the same time as its entire destiny and individuality, under the jurisdiction of practical reason, which at last is being illuminated by science and, in any case, wielded rationally by scholars and by the people themselves.

We see then the interest of these political studies of general sociology, but we see also their place. They crown and conclude our science. We thus excuse ourselves for not putting them at the conclusion; we also excuse ourselves for not having sufficiently developed them. Moreover, many other parts of sociology need to be developed also.

Chapter 2

On the Proportions of the Parts of Sociology

We also apologise for assigning to the various parts of sociology the proportions allowed to them in the *Année sociologique*, in these volumes as in those of the preceding series.

One should not reproach Durkheim for having failed to perceive this lack of harmony. No one was more aware of it than he; no one tried less to conceal it in his writings. In his teaching and in private conversations, Durkheim marked with particular care the gaps in his own knowledge and in sociological knowledge in general. If he was not generous with suggestions and information, it was not in order to mask these weaknesses, but rather to arouse vocations, enthusiasms and researches, to engage new minds in new paths, to conquer the terrain. One of the purest joys of his life was the one he felt when André Durkheim decided to penetrate for sociology the intricacies of linguistics and, under the auspices of A. Meillet, began to study what is perhaps the most extensive social phenomenon: language. Likewise, the most enduring sorrows he felt after his son's death were those occasioned by the loss of his other young collaborators. They were going to open up new pathways in his science; by their death he lost not only friends but also with them there disappeared great intellectual hopes. For they were all, with him, keen to fill gaps, to make of sociology a compact and solid system, to give it a balance like that manifested by the part of nature with which it deals.

The four social sciences which we have most neglected are those that we group under the formless heading of 'miscellaneous'. In this part of the *Année*, everything not only lacks order, as we have just seen, but proportion as well.

First, *social morphology*, already very badly located, is still almost misperceived by us. Durkheim often explained the degree to which morphology, the study of the physical structure of societies, forms the point of departure as well as the terminus of all studies of social life. It is necessary, however, once more here to contrast the small place that it occupies in these volumes with the great place that it occupies in our minds. Two considerable sciences are included within it: demography and anthropogeography or human geography, if we accept current terminology. Demography is entirely sociological; the other, at least a major part of it, is in our province; in our personal view it is entirely so, but we shall not make a major issue out of this question. We pay homage to flourishing studies and when one wishes them to develop, there is no need to quibble about words rather than about the facts with which historians or geographers concern themselves, e.g., L. Febvre, or geographers such as A. Demangeon and J. Russell Smith. Meanwhile, the reunion of these two sciences, much too widely separated at present, will lead to new advances. On the other hand, a certain number of problems until now regarded as purely demographic involve sociology in its entirety. For example, the problem of the birth rate obviously involves the structure, indeed the functioning, of the family and not only purely biological factors. The problems of morbidity or the death rate, for example, or the impact of climate on public health, do not arise identically in cities and in the countryside, nor in different social classes. Finally, let us list some more of the principal morphological phenomena: the problem, so important at the present moment, of the alterations in structure: losses of human substance as a consequence of war or famine, destructions of entire societies, the beginnings of other societies, major human currents of immigration and emigration; the distribution between town and country in constant variation; the increase in communications within and between societies; the transfers of forces; and also, henceforth, the question of shares and international transports of forces. All these problems presuppose not only the demography and geography of societies, but also knowledge of their total life. But demography – like human geography and like sociology itself – is only beginning to skim the surface of these major subjects. Moreover, their study is not yet sufficiently articulated. We shall return a third time to this subject of social morphology. Methodologically, it is essential.

The other three parts of the heading 'miscellaneous' in the *Année sociologique* equally suffer from this lack of proportion. Indeed, our own studies and the whole of sociology feel the effects of the weakness and the small quantity of works which are devoted to linguistics, technology and aesthetics. The slight attention that we can give them is truly painful. On some points, major results have been achieved and science has made notable and happy advances: in general linguistics, thanks particularly to A. Meillet and his students; in aesthetics, music and poetry, thanks particularly to E.M. von Hornbostel and Heinz Werner; in modern technologies, thanks to von Gottl-Ottlilienfeld. We should have liked to record them better. This default is entirely involuntary on our part; it would have disappeared if Bianconi, Gelly, André Durkheim and others were still with us. It is necessary, however, to repeat clearly: in social systems, whether primitive or developed, the three groups of phenomena – linguistic, technological, and aesthetic – occupy a place which is infinitely greater than the one we have given them here.

In the first place, the *linguistic phenomenon* is more general and more characteristic of social life than any other phenomenon of social physiology. As a rule, all other activities of society find their expression in it; it condenses their basic premises, and it transmits their traditions. In it there lies the majority of the notions and priorities of collectivities. This does not mean that a society contains nothing but what can be expressed in words. Some very important categories of thought can govern a multitude of acts and ideas and yet correspond to nothing which is grammatical, sometimes even to nothing which is logical, sometimes even to nothing expressed. Thus the categories of sex, or gender, are not predominant in numerous languages of societies where, nevertheless, they rule both mythology and philosophy and indeed the division of technical labour and sometimes the very location of things and persons. We are alluding to China and the Chinese, and to Polynesian societies in general. However, while the 'social' is not necessarily conscious or verbal, surely everything which is 'verbal' is conscious and social. A more important point: everything which is verbal exhibits to a very high degree, frequently to a higher degree than any other practice or collective representation, the singular character and specific character which individualises each civilisation and each society: it is essentially the creation of a community. That is to say that it is at once of the order of the general and, at the same time, of the particular. For it is general among all the individuals of that community who use the word, speak the language, and consequently think in that way; but it is common only among them; and on the other hand, each individual utters this sound, interprets the phenomenon and speaks in his own fashion, so that his language is, so to speak, ordinarily the average and occasionally the ideal. It is therefore the common means and consequently the natural and first means by which men define their thought and their action; and at the same time it bears in a high degree the mark of the artificial and the arbitrary. Moreover, apart even from the major interest of its study in itself, since language contains as much action as representation, it raises, more than ideas or institutions, whether these be religious or moral, the capital problem of the relations between ideation and action in social consciousness. This is a problem that no one has dared to tackle, and perhaps will not dare to tackle for a long time. Meanwhile, the materials are beginning to arrive ready for exploitation. For example, by linking the work of Henri Hubert on the concept of time with the work of Marcel Cohen on the expression of time in the Semitic verb one can believe in or glimpse the possibility, that perhaps one day it will be possible to attack the general problem using these two approaches.

In any case, when the problems raised by that part of linguistics which is social or, more exactly, that part of sociology which is linguistic, have surpassed the fragmentary or preliminary stage, at that point one might perhaps recast both general sociology and linguistic sociology in particular. Many other parts of sociology would feel the effects, for example, the theories of poetic aesthetics, of prayer, and even of legal and proverbial formulas. We accept that this magnificent field awaits its specialised workers. The linguists are kindly measuring it out for us, and Meillet will continue to clear away the underbrush; but we know well that the sociology of language constitutes, like social morphology, if not a fundamental and self-sufficient division by itself, at least a division of social facts that is more general than the other five divisions, for religion, morality, economy, aesthetics and technology are crystallised in it. They are transmitted more or less entirely in language even though this latter has a certain autonomy towards them.

The dimension of the *aesthetic phenomenon*, insofar as it is social, is considerable in itself and with respect to other social phenomena. The relative sise of the sociology of aesthetics is perhaps even more notable in relation to other divisions to which we seem to attribute more importance. Unfortunately we have never been able to bring the importance of the topic into the full light of day. Durkheim made more than an allusion to it in his *Elementary Forms of the Religious Life*, and we have endeavoured never to lose sight of it in the *Année*. It is true that others have rather exaggerated it, as, for example, the old master Wundt, when he puts rhythm at the base of language, art at the origin of myth, and when, despite his transcendentalism, he puts myth and aesthetic representation at the origin of religion. In general, however, sociologists direct their interest more to the classical problems of morality, the economy, and religion, no further, and the role of the aesthetic phenomenon is underestimated.

However, the phenomena of the life of art are, perhaps after those of language, the ones which have most largely surpassed their *limit* at least in the civilisations which have preceded ours. Only in the completely modern period and still in restricted circles has art for art's sake become a principle. In other civilisations, and no doubt it will be the same in future civilisations, art serves for everything and colours everything. In religion the rhythm of the poetry and music, the poetry and music themselves, the theatrical combination, the dance, the fine image, reproduced, mimed or even dreamed, play an immense role; in morality, it is etiquette, propriety, elegance, and beauty of manners which are striven for equally with duties and rituals. The majority of needs or rather tastes, and consequently the scale of economic values, and in further consequence the techniques themselves, are commanded by the sense of beauty, or that which is physiologically good; we speak for example of cuisine. And so on. The fine arts, to adopt the popular distinction which Espinas has rendered profound, are therefore, like arts or techniques, a phenomenon characteristic of life in the community, and not simply of a part of that life. They are indeed more typical of societies than their crafts. Their domain is one of the broadest, extending into all the others, whereas technology seems historically to be one of the first domains to have closed itself off in its own sphere.

Technology. Even though one of us, Henri Hubert, archaeologist and prehistorian, is by profession a student of technology, we have never had the necessary time and energy to give to technology the formidable place which it merits.

'Homo faber' says Bergson. These formulae signify only the obvious or they signify too much, because the choice of such a sign hides other equally obvious signs. This formula has the merit, however, of reclaiming for technology a place of honor in the history of humanity. It recalls a forgotten philosophy. And we would happily adopt it, along with others, on one condition: that it denote, not a 'creative power' which too much resembles the 'dormitive force' of opium, but a characteristic feature of communal life, and not of the individual and profound life of the mind. A practical art has two roots – the invention of the movement or the implement, and the tradition of its use, indeed the use itself – and in both respects it is essentially a social thing, as we have known since Noiré, the colleague of Nietzsche, whose philosophical works are still important in this part of our science. The point, however, which has never been sufficiently developed is the degree to which all of social life depends upon technology.

Nevertheless, three groups of scholars know it. First of all, the prehistorians and the archeologists. These scholars, basically, even in their oldest classifications of so-called 'races' or 'ages' (which in reality were of civilisations and societies), arrange them and their contacts only according to the order of succession and the types of their industries – evidence of this kind being in any case almost the only visible traces of these people.

The ethnographers also proceed in this fashion. We indicated last year, and we shall return to the subject on various occasions in the present volume, and certainly in the following volumes, – the legitimate fashion in which attempts are being made at present to write, particularly with the aid of technological criteria, the history of societies reputedly without history. With reference to special problems, we shall weigh the value of this sign among other signs. In any case, ethnographers know that the history of industry is an important aspect of human history. Among the ethnologists, therefore, technology has a great and essential role which corresponds to the profound nature of techniques.

Lastly come the technologists properly so-called: those who study modern techniques, industry and its historical and conceptual development. Their science made a tangible advance when M. von Gottl-Ottlilienfeld published his *Technology*, in the excellent *Grundriss der Sozialökonomik* (cf. *Année*, n.s. 1). This work, a handbook but of profound originality, marks an era. And even although it appears in a series on political economy, it proclaims and justifies the rights of that whole new science, which deserves to be set free and to acquire major importance. Moreover, a long time has elapsed since the American technologists and ethnographers, Otis T. Mason among others, all those who followed Powell, the profound and original founder of the Bureau of Ethnology, proclaimed that technology was a special and very eminent part of sociology. They did this independently of the German scholars, Bastian and his students. Unfortunately, this tradition weakened in Germany as in England. This science, however, has once again begun to enjoy respect. Surely people will continue to extend and to deepen the study of modern technologies. At the same time, efforts will be made to write not a detailed history, which is almost always impossible, but a typological history of the tradition of human crafts and human labour. Now at last it is possible to link up the ideas of Reuleau, the German founder of a purely mechanical technology, with the ideas of Powell, founder of an ethnographical technology. There is a brilliant future for this science. We cannot estimate it, even approximately.

For technology presents not only an intrinsic interest as a special form of social activity and as a specific form of the general activity of mankind. It also presents an interest from a general point of view. In fact, like language or the fine arts, the techniques of a society exhibit the characteristic of being many things at once. First, they are particular to a single society, or at least to a single civilisation, to the point of characterising it, indeed of standing for it, so to say, like a sign. Nothing manifests more the difference between two social traditions than the difference, still enormous even in our days, between the implements and the crafts of two societies. The method of handling and the forms of implements which they imply, of two peoples as close as the French and the English, are still almost absurd. There are different spades and shovels, and this difference requires differences in the mode of their use, and vice versa. It is enough to make one doubt Reason. One should read in Ssu-Ma-Ch'en, the oldest Chinese historian, how the Court and the Office of Rites debated the question of whether, together with the use of chariots, China should or should not adopt the style of the Huns when mounting a horse. Like all social phenomena, then, techniques are on one side arbitrary and particular to the community which invents them. Etymologically, 'artificial' comes from art and from artifice, 'technique' derives from (Greek) *techné*. At the same time, however, more than any other social phenomenon, the arts are apt to cross the boundaries of societies. Techniques are eminently liable to borrowing. From the oldest epochs of humanity, from the so-called lower palaeolithic, tools and procedures have travelled. Indeed, they are the principal object of commerce and imitation. Everywhere they are the expansive social thing *par excellence*. By their nature, techniques tend to be generalised and to multiply everywhere throughout humanity. They are the most important of the factors in the causes, means, and the ends of what is called civilisation, and also of progress, not only social but human. Here is why. Religion, law, and the economy are limited to each society, a little more or a little less than language, but comparably. Even when they are propagated, they are only means by which the community acts on itself. In contrast, techniques are the means, this time physical, which a society possesses to act upon its milieu. Through techniques, man increasingly becomes master of the earth and its products. They are, then, a compromise between nature and humanity. From this fact, through this extraordinary extrasocial position, they have a general and human nature. That miracle, the instrument; that double miracle, that compounding of instruments, the machine; that triple miracle, the compounding of machines, industry; like the rest of social life, these miracles have thus raised man above himself, but at the same time they have taken him out of himself. Here again, *homo* is *duplex*, but he is so in a different sense than in law or religion. In religious ecstasy, in moral sacrifice, around the Golden Calf, man and society always remain themselves with their limits and imperfections. In practical arts, man makes his limits recede. He advances in nature, at the same time as above his proper nature, because he adjusts it to nature. He identifies himself with the mechanical, physical and chemical order of things. He creates and at the same time he creates himself; he creates at once his means of living, things purely human, and his thought written in these things. Here true practical reason is elaborated.

Technology and natural history of the sciences. Perhaps it is also in techniques and in relation to them that true reason itself is elaborated. We must recognise that the plan proposed and our studies themselves present a very serious gap on this point, the most serious perhaps among those which concern the special parts of sociology. Contrary to the Comtean tradition, we nowhere study for itself the natural and social history of the sciences. It is not that we lack support. The distinguished editors of *Isis: Review of the History of Sciences*, Abel Rey and others, also conceive their work as eminently sociological. Nevertheless, until now, we have not made an effort to assign a place to these studies, still less to estimate their extent and depth. Some observations are therefore necessary here.

When the arts and the sciences and their historical relations are studied concretely, the division between pure reason and practical reason seems scholastic, scarcely realistic, barely psychological, and even less sociological. We know, we see, we feel the profound links which unite them in their raisons d'être and in their history. Particularly strong at the origin, they are still obvious today when, in a thousand cases, technology poses the questions which science resolves and often creates the facts which science mathematicises or schematises after the fact. On the other hand, quite often, theoretical discovery proposes the phenomenon, the principle, or the invention which industry then exploits. The scientific-technical complex is a single bloc. For example, the oldest calendars are as much the work of farmers as of religious minds or of astrologers; technique, science, and myth are there blended. In the same way, pigeons had been selectively bred before Darwin found the notion of natural selection. The same is true of pure and experimental science – which in our days replaces mythologies, metaphysics and pure action, even action based on reflection; it is not in the least disengaged from the action which it directs, even when it detaches itself most clearly or most deliberately. Have not the most modern doctrines of cosmology finally led to purely practical researches? Attempts are made to find a stable measure in the single constant known at present: the length of a light wave.

Here then is the reason why the history of sciences and epistemology perhaps needs to be situated in a special part of the sociology of technology. In fact, science is the other social activity which, like technology, draws man out of himself towards nature and which inspires that technology and which has the same goal, namely control over things.

Nevertheless, we hesitate before this radical solution. This arrangement neglects a specific difference. In his industrial arts, man remains man and only half emerges from himself. In contrast, science makes him emerge completely, and has identified him with things. Once engaged in science, he is aware of things in and for themselves, rather than feeling them exclusively in relation to himself and to his acts, or of representing them in a kind of magic mirror, in relation to mythical images, sometimes useless ones.

And from this there arises a second difference between sciences and techniques. However expansive and imitable techniques may be, they are, even in our day, relatively variable between nations. In contrast, while science remains social insofar as it is due to the collaboration and controlled verification by humans, it nevertheless ceases to be the work of societies as such. More and more it is the treasure of the entire human community and no longer of any particular society. Having formerly been fashioned from jealous traditions, secrets and mysteries, alchemies and recipes, it is now something in broad daylight and belonging to humanity. In order to approach its study, perhaps it is necessary to adopt immediately not the partial viewpoint of past or present societies, but rather the viewpoint of the greatest possible society – humanity. For these last two reasons it may be necessary to add epistemology as a new division to sociology.

On the other hand, perhaps it is preferable to leave science to its natural connection: geometrical, mechanical, physical and chemical practical activity on things, and also rational practice on animate creatures and humans, the agricultural, veterinarian and medical arts. Indeed, it might be better, like Espinas and the Greeks he followed, not to distinguish *techné* and *epistémé*. Perhaps, like Durkheim, one should separate them profoundly without contrasting them. We could balance the pros and the cons endlessly; we open the debate and we do not know how to close it. Like the good Pindar, we do not know what is just.

From the place which we assign to it, however, one can see how far the problems of science and technology are fundamental and condition the problem of the social origins of reason. And, let it be said in passing, here is an additional motive for putting this branch at the end and not at the beginning of our studies.

* * *

Even within the framework of the old divisions of the *Année sociologique*, some just and well-disposed critics note the disequilibria and disproportions of which

Durkheim was always aware. Here, for example, in the science of religions, we study, perhaps too much, the 'primitives' and not enough our own major religions, and the movements of feelings and ideas which agitate them. There, in economic science or politics, we perhaps give too little attention to ancient ethnography and history. In addition, we make too little use of quantitative methods; but one can measure attendance at churches and cinemas, as well as the totals of working hours, errors in the postal service, or the ages of suicides. We ourselves follow fashions or the state of our sciences. Whether rightly or wrongly, the history of religion is completely oriented towards the past and is not accustomed to breaking down statistics, whereas political economy is a science of numbers, entirely oriented towards the present, indeed towards the future, and forgetting perhaps too much the past or the societies which surround us. Finally, we follow our tastes and our capacities. We do not, and we should not, hide the fact. We are far from the ideal and we frankly acknowledge it.

A sociology and an *Année sociologique* better organised and better proportioned are the first well-defined goal that we pursue. May the new effort that we are all making here garner for us the approval of young workers; collaborating with us, may they find and determine the lacunae in our knowledge, extend their own, and find abstractions that offer a better fit to the body of social phenomena.

Up until now, the image that we give of this body remains a caricature. In the absence of sufficient studies of morphology, one could say that, according to us, society is a body without feet; for lack of linguistics, one could say without language; lacking aesthetics and technology, one could believe that we see it without senses and without arms; without a systematic study of the collective consciousness, one could say it has no soul. One could believe that, as our neighbours do with their British 'social anthropology', we know only *homo religiosus, ethicus, economicus*.

These criticisms are not designed to ruin the method of division that we have followed and are still following. They are meant to compensate the inevitable defects presented by the divisions into compartments with which it was necessary to begin. We have to see what they are worth. Their principal disadvantage is that they prevent us from treating otherwise than by generalities two fundamental questions: (1) social relations and collective ethology; (2) the collective consciousness.

Collective ethology, the study of the characters or the souls of societies, has remained literary and historical. The reason for this is that it is above all a study of relations among *all* social phenomena. The separate social sciences and the special sociologies prevent a clear view of these relations.

Even less obvious than the order and the proportion of all these divisions is the relation which they sustain among themselves. Ideally we should know each of these relations in particular and even the relation in general – if there exists something which is the essence of social relations – and all the relations in general. In other words, we should know what they have which is singular in each known society and at the same time what they have that is general in all known societies, in order to be able to infer from the known societies to all possible societies or to be able to classify and soundly appraise a given society, and consequently to direct it. We have made little progress on this subject. We do not know either what constitutes the character or the singularity of each society, nor how each society is composed (apart from the humans and the land which constitute it) from states of mind [*âme*] and practical habits, which are comparable from top to bottom of the scale of the history of societies. Nor do we know why each society is individually different from another, nor do we glimpse why these institutions and these movements, these ideas and these groups nevertheless obey laws or, if one prefers, necessary relations – relations which, to phrase it better, are general and intelligible. For two facts dominate the natural history of societies. In all societies we find phenomena of the same sort, those studied by the different special sociologies and general sociology. However, these phenomena of various kinds appear differently proportioned and differently coloured in each society. Throughout the whole of human progress, in the genealogy of societies, the dimension of each has varied; and in this immense medley of their simultaneous and successive variations – in this kaleidoscope of their constantly-changing arrangements – resides the secret of that *mélange* which is particular to each society at each moment, which gives it an aspect and, in each of its eras, so to speak, a special style or aspect. It is the mystery of these relations and these *mélanges* that must be sought, and this is what the history of each society does seek. We are poorly prepared to enter upon that path, and provide a good description of the individuality of each society. And for the same reason we are badly prepared to fashion a general theory of social relations, a theory of the social 'relation'. So the bringing together of all these mysteries and all these similarities must be the setting point towards this ideal science of societies which will explain, or rather understand, the general and the particular in each of them. For a general theory of this particularity can be attempted, and Durkheim proposed to call it 'collective ethology'. These two parts – ethology and a theory of social relations – are equally necessary.

From the point of view of the classical divisions, the last problem is equally difficult to pose, that of the very nature of the collective conscience, whether this be active and reflective or passive and mechanical. Here our expressions, even to us, too often still remain abstract and general: some readers even thought that Durkheim substantialised the collective conscience. Nothing is more dangerous than to speak of *society*, when one means to describe *societies*, conscious minds thinking together, the psychic things of some particular social life – what is properly the collective conscience. Besides, Durkheim had clearly characterised collective representations; we have indeed isolated a certain number of these collective representations; we are carefully considering the parts. It is still necessary to consider the whole that these compose, the collective conscienceness. Just as psychologically a human thinks, intends, acts and feels, all at once, with his whole body, so that community of bodies and minds which is a society feels, acts, lives and wishes to live with all the bodies and all the minds of all these humans. It is their totality, the totality of these totalities; it is that and nothing else, and that is enough. As is clear then, a concrete science should indeed, after having divided, re-embrace all its divisions. In this way it will be possible – perhaps by calling on other sciences, the biological sciences in particular, rather than the psychological sciences – to arrive at a science of the body and soul of societies. From this point of view, the complete problem of collective conscienceness and reason can perhaps be approached objectively. For example, rather than studying human reason from some sides only, or in bits and pieces, as we nearly all have done, we shall study it in relation to the totality of rhythms, acts and forces in the entire society. On top of researches which are excessively limited in their scope, even when they surpass simple analysis, we shall superimpose a synthesis which will endeavour to be complete.

If our science thus seems to be marking time before these serious problems, and before others which we do not even glimpse, this probably stems from a single cause. We have had to divide up in order to begin to understand, but that is not all we have. Basically, we are still in the rut of abstraction and prejudgment, impotent to depart from the narrow classifications imposed upon us by the already ancient sciences of economics, law, religion, etc., surely respectable sciences but still in their infancy; our divisions which follow them are, like them, surely faulty. Ultimately we are not certain that they exhaust reality. This partition is too limiting and too precise in its listing. The headings of 'general sociology' and 'miscellaneous' which we use mask this inability to arrive at the necessary precision and betray our insecurity. In addition, the names of the special sociologies themselves correspond too closely to the way in which modern social labour or the activities of our Western societies are divided up; these divisions are more contemporary and more ephemeral than is usually recognised. Thus, they bear profoundly the mark of our own times and our subjectivity. They fit badly with the life of those societies which have divided their work differently or with the life of those societies which will one day divide it otherwise than we do. Finally, excessively empirical on some points, they fragment and divide, and because they divide and isolate excessively, they abstract and continue to produce a fragmented and mutilated image of reality.

There is thus a temptation to overturn this whole compartmentalisation of social phenomena, to bring down this edifice of special sociologies. That would be imprudent and useless. The edifice may be allowed to subsist, because in this direction the science is still very far from having completed its journey.

No doubt, there is a solution to all of these problems. There may exist other rational and real divisions, valid for all known societies. It is probably necessary to superimpose on our divisions, or rather to oppose to them, symmetrically and complementarily, another division of the same phenomena of the common life which is clearer and at the same time more concrete. The same facts will be included, but now seen from a different angle. In our opinion, this consideration, which starts from a different point of view, is necessary.

Long ago, in his *Rules of Sociological Method*, Durkheim proposed another division of social phenomena, symmetrical with the division of biology into morphology and physiology. Unfortunately, he was never able to expound at sufficient length the principle of this division, but the following chapter is largely based on his conversations. This bipartite division of social phenomena into morphological and physiological is perhaps the true division, if not the only one. Perhaps new generations of workers will set off on in this path; but this need not prevent the older workers from continuing in their old way. However, since it is not in common use, let us emphasise this method and the necessity for using it.

Chapter 3

Concrete Divisions of Sociology

I. The Principle

Factually, there are only two things in a society: (1) *the group* which forms it, ordinarily on a specific portion of the earth's surface; and (2) *the representations and the movements* of this group. This is to say that on one side there are only material phenomena: finite numbers of individuals of particular ages, at some definite moment and at some specific location; and on the other side, amongst the ideas and the actions of these humans which are common to them, those which are at the same time the effect of their life in common. There is nothing else. The first phenomenon, i.e., the group and the things, corresponds to *morphology*, the study of material structures;[1] the second phenomenon corresponds to *social physiology*, i.e., the study of these structures in movement, in other words, their functions and the functioning of these functions. Durkheim divided the latter precisely into the *physiology of practices* and the *physiology of collective representations*.

While this is not certainly true of the division that we ordinarily follow, that of the special sociologies, this division is complete beyond any doubt. It may well also be exact, for it is profoundly concrete. It divides nothing but what obviously is divided. In a word, it leaves things as they should be.

* * *

In principle it follows the divisions of biology and of psychology.

Nevertheless, this imitation of biology must not be pushed too far, for the distinction drawn between morphologists and physiologists in biology is itself not without its dangers. These borrowings of methods, from one science to another, must be carried out with prudence. As an object lesson, let us recall

Comte's absurd error, when he borrowed from mechanics his distinction between social statics and social dynamics. And let us see the things under the words. For we are using terms that Durkheim borrowed thirty years ago from sciences that have subsequently advanced and these terms must be defined. The primary division into morphology and physiology should be cut free from all overtones of the life sciences. These words cannot even have the same meaning in sociology as in other sciences. We must specify precisely the meaning we give them. Thus we shall accentuate the general lines of this plan of sociology, before showing its advantages.

The contents of social morphology. This division remains the same as in our accustomed plan. Social morphology is basically the best-constituted of all the parts of sociology, and in it the two plans coincide. But it follows from that that it should not be understood simply like animal or vegetable morphologies.

Even more than in the case of an organism, from which an immobilising stroke of the scalpel can isolate a tissue, or from which dissection can resect an organ, a society exists in time, in movement and in the mind. Even its material structure is in such a perpetual state of flux, or rather a snapshot would capture so many different ages, the two sexes, and so many different origins, that any attempt to separate movement from structure or anatomy from physiology would necessarily remain on a purely abstract level. There are even societies, as we have shown, which have several structures succeeding one another with the seasons. Others are composed of various elements, some of which themselves have different and variable structures, e.g., a maritime population, where the men are frequently far away, or groups of vagabonds (like those quaintly labelled 'hobos' in America), who spend the winters in cities; also, elsewhere, what is called more technically the floating population; all these kinds of groups, and many others, should be studied in themselves and in their movements. Likewise, the study of a city cannot be separated from its history nor from the origins of its population. In a word, if humans group themselves into societies, villages and hordes, it is because they wish to do so and also because ideas intervene here too. Social morphology, then, should not be compared only with the morphology familiar to biologists.

Let us say then, using other words, that it studies the group qua material phenomenon. (Cf. Durkheim, *Année Sociologique*, II, 520 et seq.) It includes and should embrace in itself everything which is confused or arbitrarily divided under the rubrics of: statistics (exception made for (1) special statistics which relate to the study of institutions – moral, economic, etc.; and (2) somatic statistics of stature, etc., which relate to somatological anthropology); *demography*; *human geography* or anthropogeography or historical geography or political and economic geography. It also includes the study of the movements of population in time and in space: birth rates, death rates, age; alternative structures and fluctuating ones; displacement and migratory currents. It also includes the study of the subgroups of the society insofar as these have associated with the territory. Someday a complete sociology will be built on this solid base. And this very large base, of masses and numbers, can be graphically depicted, at the same time as it can be mathematically measured. Social morphology, then, is one of the most compact parts of sociology; the conclusions it can supply are the most mentally satisfying ones.

The contents of social physiology. Apart from the humans and the things contained in a society, there exist in it only the shared representations and the shared acts of these humans – not all the facts they share, such as eating and sleeping, but only those which are the effect of their life in society. This category of facts is the life of the society. It constitutes a system of functions and their functioning. So it is still structure, but structure in motion. But above all, since we are dealing with facts of consciousness at the same time as material facts, they are also facts of mental and moral life. They can therefore be divided into two categories: (1) *social acts*, or *social practices*, or *institutions*, when the acts are traditional and are repeated by virtue of tradition; (2) the *collective ideas* and *sentiments* which preside over or correspond to these acts, or at least are the object of collective beliefs. This division of the facts corresponds with the division of social physiology into: (1) the *physiology of practices*, (2) the *physiology of representations*.

One can see why, as with the word *morphology*, the word *physiology* should be employed with caution. The word is still impregnated with biological abstraction and it should not reawaken the metaphor of the social organism. Finally, while it expresses well the idea of the life and the movement of humans in societies – in reality, the physiology of the *mores*, practices, acts and social currents – the word is wrong in the sense that it does not clearly express what there is of the conscious, sentimental, ideal, voluntary and arbitrary in the surges and the traditions of those human collectivities that constitute societies.

At this point it would be easy to speak of collective psychology rather than of social physiology. From one point of view, indeed, this would be an advance. The expression neatly emphasises that this entire part of sociology is essentially psychological, that everything is expressed there in terms of consciousness, of psychology if you prefer – provided that it is clearly understood that the latter form communities of conscious minds, that they are conscious minds living in common, controlling common action, forming among themselves a common milieu. This is what social psychology can mean. However, if all social physiology is thus reduced, the entire material portion of the facts of physiology would disappear from view: the transformation of ideas and sentiments into acts and movements of individuals, their perpetuation in crafted or manufactured objects, etc., even their frequency. And all the research would be gravely distorted. In effect, one would be letting slip from consideration *the two characteristics* by which every social fact is distinguished from facts of individual psychology: (1) *it is statistical and can be counted* (we repeat this observation and will return to it again), being common to definite numbers of humans during specific periods; and (2) (which is included) *it is historical*. With reference to this latter sign, it is well to specify that every social fact is a moment in the history of a group of humans, that it is the end and commencement of one or several series. So let us simply say: every social fact, including the acts of the conscious mind, is a fact of life. The word *physiology* is comprehensive; it prejudges nothing; let us retain it.

Moreover, just as we have endeavoured to cleanse the word *physiology* of all biological overtones, let us similarly endeavour to preserve this division of social physiology itself, between the physiology of collective acts and the physiology of collective representations; let us try to cleanse it of all compromising psychological overtones. Indeed, since Münsterberg, the corresponding classification in psychology has been the object of impassioned discussions. If we use it, we do so in the name of common usage. Sociology has an interest in borrowing only words belonging to the current language, but it must give them a meaning that is precise and specific to the discipline. Words of this kind produce only slight inconvenience, if what they connote is known precisely. In the social realm, everything is situated on another level, according to other symmetries, with other affinities than in the realm of individual consciousness. Thus the terms *acts* and *representations* do not have the same value, and the contrast between the facts which they designate does not have the same significance as in psychology.

The interweaving of movement and representation is greater in social life. In fact, a punishment, a suicide, a temple, an implement, are material facts, like commerce or war. Nevertheless, they are also moral or religious, technical, economic, or general facts. The behaviour of man as a social being is therefore even more linked to the collective consciousness than individual behaviour is linked to the individual consciousness. A social act is always motivated. Ideas can dominate, indeed, to the point of negating individuals' lives, even ending in the destruction of peoples or groups, e.g., a hopeless siege, or the last-ditch resistance of a platoon of machinegunners. Conversely, by virtue of being social, a phenomenon is nearly always an act, or an attitude that is taken. Even the negation of an act – a peace, the absence of war – is a thing; to live without lawsuits is agreeable; a taboo, a negative ritual, a prescription of etiquette, is an act – if I do not pass you, it is because I hold back from walking. Even the most elevated collective representations have no existence, are not truly such, except insofar as they command acts. Whatever may be said by the theologians of some churches, of some heresies, and by some literary men who take words for facts, faith is nothing without works. It is in itself a work, i.e., the search for a mental condition, for confidence, for a revelation. Even among the extreme quietists it implies the taking of an attitude – namely quietism itself, that negative behaviour which some would wish to be present as an idea, but which consists in voluntarily emptying the soul of all acts and perhaps of every idea.

This intimate link between act and representation is inevitable as soon as we leave the realm of pure mystical theory and come to social facts. There is a reason for this, namely, the collective character, and consequently the statistical character, of social facts. Such facts necessarily occur one or more times among a plurality of individuals living in society. Consequently, something is not surely collective, even when it is a pure representation, unless it is materialised to a certain degree, sometimes quite remotely; for example, in a book, or in a collectivity's behavior. Conversely, nowhere, even in art and in the most idle exercise of mysticism and the imagination or in so-called pure science – nowhere is there either ideation or *sentimentalisation* [*Einfuhlung*] worthy of designation as 'collective' unless there is at least some communication or language; unless there is a minimum of collective acts, repetitions, imitations, authority, and, let us add, without a minimal frequency of images represented to minds, simultaneous or identical apprehensions of certain aspects or certain forms [*Gestalt*] of things, of the ideas and acts that form the object of the collective representation. Thus, in sociology as in psychology, we are certain that there is a representation only when there is behaviour. But also, in sociology more certainly than in psychology, even behaviour that is negative and purely inhibitory is not a pure tropism. What is true in psychology is a hundred times more so in sociology, and even more verifiable, since we know from experience that the conduct of our fellow citizens has the same *raisons d'être* as our own, insofar as it is of social importance. Thus, instead of opposing representation and act, as is commonly done, we shall say rather representation and behaviour, collective representation and collective behaviour. Only exceptionally shall we isolate one from the other.

We must agree that this division of social physiology into the physiology of acts and the physiology of representations should not be considered as a rule. It is simple, clear, distinct, and provisionally necessary for us. This does not prove that it is adequate to all the material under study. In the present state of psychology and sociology, we can only contrast the social movements of humans – which belong to the realm of matter, time and space, like the bodies and the other movements of the bodies of individuals – and the social consciousness, the states of social consciousness which exist in that society – or rather the collective representations which are to be found among the individuals grouped there. Thus the psychologist abstracts body movements from the thought which they express. However, the concrete phenomenon, in its completeness, is a unity: body and soul. In most cases, the question raided by a social fact, for example, by the promulgation of a statute, bears not only on the collective concepts and sentiments on the one hand, nor only on the acts and their sanctions on the other; it bears on the relationship between the two, and even more on those facts which go beyond this relationship, for example, on the ideal and the normal, on the averages and the realities that one can number in that society, but which we still understand very poorly.

II. Advantages of this Division

Subject to the reservations just expressed, this division of sociology does not offer any disadvantage. It is disengaged from all metaphysics and from all impure mixture with other sciences. It contradicts nothing, because it can and should be employed concurrently with the division into general sociology and the special sociologies, if only to verify and cross-check research at every moment. These two divisions necessarily tolerate one another. We shall even see how the latter permits us to find a way back to the division into the special sociologies. In a word, it offers nothing but advantages.

The leading one of these, to repeat the point, is that the division is complete. It omits nothing. In a collectivity there are obviously only three groups of collective phenomena: the mass of individuals, their acts, and their ideas.

The division is clear and distinct. It does not divide anything which is not perfectly divided in reality.

It may also be more exact than any other, more adapted to the facts. The reason is that it is profoundly and exclusively concrete, based only on manifest signs: a material structure, the movements of groups, actions – all this is visible; the representations of individuals in groups – this is spoken about and known, and even is visible through social practices.

Finally, there is no need to be affronted by the abstract terms which we employ – this division, all-inclusive this time, is eminently realistic. It presents reality at one stroke. What needs to be described, what is given at each instant, is a social whole integrating individuals who are themselves wholes. For an example, let us take an important moral fact. We shall even select one of those which may not be repeated. For there do exist extraordinary social facts, non-traditional facts in the life of societies. A major emigration, a war, a panic, are events which lack neither the historical character nor the statistical character of the social fact. They are at once morphological, dynamic and cognitive. Let us descend even to the level of historical and statistical analysis of the particular cases comprehended in a moral phenomenon, such as suicide; let us consider a particular type of suicide, of some particular type of person, of some particular age group, in some particular societies. One thus almost comes to reach the individual in its completeness. Similarly too, a phenomenon that we have recently studied (*Journal de Psychologie*, 1926), the collective suggestion of death (what happens in certain populations where humans let themselves die because they believe they have sinned or because they believe themselves bewitched) shows unadorned not only the morality and the religiosity of these humans, but also the relationship they have with life itself and the desire for death. Thus sociology encounters the biological totality. What sociology always and everywhere observes is not the human divided into psychological or even into sociological compartments, but the entire human being. By following a parallel method in the division of the facts, this real and ultimate element is recovered.

Finally, such a plan poses problems in terms of pure sociology, i.e., in terms of number, space and time, in terms of the nature of ideas and of actions, and finally and most particularly in terms of relationships and functions. Thereby, it clarifies the nature of sociology and renders its domain more delicately and with better definition.

For what is true of the special functions of the organs of a living body is even more true, and furthermore is true in quite another sense, of the functions and functionings in a human society. Everything in it consists entirely of relationships, and this applies even to the material nature of things: an implement is nothing if it is not used. Let us return to our familiar example. An industry is not only a technical thing, but must be considered from all kinds of other points of view. It only exists because it generates economic profit, because it responds to a market and to prices; it is localised in one place or another for reasons that are geographic or purely demographic or even political or traditional; the economic administration of this industry belongs to some individual for legal reasons; it can relate only in the fine arts or to sports; and so on. In a society, everything, even the most specialised things, is, and is above all, function and functioning. Nothing can be understood except in relationship to the whole, to the entire collectivity, and not in relationship to its separate parts. There is no social phenomenon which is not an integral part of the social whole. This is true not only in the way in which our foot or our hand or even some more or less essential internal organ are part of ourselves, but – although this comparison with physiological functions is still inadequate and even though the unity of sociological phenomena is still superior – in the way in which a state of consciousness or a part of our character are not separable parts of our selves, but *are* ourselves at a given moment. Every social state and all social activity, even transient, must be related to this unity, to this integrated totality, extraordinary as this entity is: the totality of distinct human bodies and the totality of consciousnesses, separated and nevertheless united – united at once by constraint and volition, by destiny and free choice. For what assembles them and makes them live in common, what makes them think and act together and in synchrony is a natural rhythm, a unanimity which is deliberately sought, even arbitrary, but is nonetheless necessary, as it always will be.

By a clear view of its subject-matter, then, the unity of sociology is justified. An appended note [see additional bibliographical note following this essay] will emphasise this unity with reference to some recent books. At this point, however, it is important to recall that this is the most productive principle in Durkheim's method. There are not *several* social sciences, but *one science of societies*. Of course, each social phenomenon must be isolated in order to study it; the explanation of one social phenomenon can be sought only in other social phenomena. These latter, however, are not necessarily from the same order (e.g., religious, moral, or technical) as the former. Indeed, they are most often of a quite different nature. Outside of social morphology, which must be distinguished and separated in order to bring its explanatory value into sharper relief, all the other sections of sociology, the special sociologies or social sciences are, from this point of view, only parts of social physiology. This latter can quite easily be divided up on the basis of the various social categories, religions or mores, economy, crafts, fine arts and games, and language. But sociology is there in order to prevent us from forgetting any of the connections. For the explanation is complete only when, over and above the physiological connections, the material and morphological connections have been described.

In other words, one should never separate from one another the various parts of sociology nor, more particularly, the parts of social physiology. Among social phenomena there exist the most varied relationships. Customs and ideas push their roots in all directions. The error is to neglect these innumerable and profound anastomoses. The principal goal of our studies is precisely to give a feeling for these extremely various linkages of cause and effect, of goals, of ideal directions and material forces (including the land and objects) which, by their interactions, form the real tissue of a society, living and ideal at the same time. This is how a concrete study of sociology, precisely like an historical study, normally always goes beyond the fields covered by a single specialty, even when they are narrowly delimited. The historian of religions, of law, and of the economy, must often go beyond the limits which he sets for himself. Nevertheless, this enlargement enriches the most narrowly delimited studies. Thus, again, one will comprehend each institution taken singly, by relating it to the whole, whereas each one isolated in its category remains a mystery if it is considered separately. The moralist will always find that we have not 'provided a foundation' for morality; the theologian, that we have not exhausted religious 'reality' or 'experience'; the economist will remain flabbergasted in the face of the 'laws' which he thought he had discovered and which are in reality nothing but some contemporary norms of action. However, the problem changes when all these parts are taken together, if one goes in turn from the whole to the parts and from the parts to the whole. One can then, honestly and fairly, express the hope that one day a science of man, even if incomplete (a biological, psychological and sociological anthropology), drawing on all the conditions in which humans have lived, will make sense of all the diverse forms, or at least the most important among the forms which have been taken by life, his activity, his affective faculties and his ideation.

* * *

Such are the general advantages of this plan of work. Each part of the plan also possesses its utility.

In particular, the division of the phenomena of social physiology has this considerable advantage: it is rigorously concrete. It allows one in general to raise all the problems with a minimum of abstraction. It never isolates collective behaviours from the corresponding collective states of consciousness. And it isolates neither the one nor the other from the statistical scale or the structure of the group where they are found.

First of all, it collects together all the representations and all the collective practices, thus paving the way for a general theory of representations and for a general theory of action. In fact, quite frequently, collective representations have more affinities and more natural connections with each other than with the various forms of social activity which specifically correspond to them one by one. A notion and a word, e.g., the idea and the word *cause*, are not only related to religion, law, techniques and language, they are the total of these relations. Indeed the idea, the entire notion of *cause* touches the philosophical notion of values, for example, in the judgements of value which constitute magic and religion, as it touches the beginnings of formal logic in divination and in procedure. One could make other observations on the notion of fault – legal, religious, and professional all at the same time – among the Maoris or even the Berbers. Myths – another example – are full of legal principles. And so on. There is danger in not perceiving and in not systematically researching these relationships.

Likewise, practices often go hand in hand and are less separated from one another than the various notions which more or less consciously preside over them. Punishment is in numerous societies quite as much as expiation or a payment as an act of justice. All ownership is an economic act, even that of a ritual. These observations might be multiplied endlessly.

Lastly, by separating better the two groups of facts which are a function of one another – namely collective representations and collective practices – this division makes more apparent the relations which unite them, particularly relations which are indirect but nevertheless intimate. It postulates that no representation is totally without a reverberation on action and that there is no pure action. Externally, a popular and traditional story is nothing but literature. Internally, when its mechanisms and its themes are analyzed, it is seen as full of the memories of ancient practices, that it corresponds to popular superstitions, with more or less living rules regarding omens, etc. In the same way, science at first glance appears as purely ideal, technology as exclusively practical. If one persists, however, in seeking for the notions which govern the one and the movements that are commanded by the other, one quickly sees that the two are dominated by a natural unity. Science directs technology which is an applied science, and technology directs science because it poses questions to it. Likewise too, from this point of view language appears as a matter immediately of action as much as of thought, perhaps even more so, and the problem debated by the linguists is posed in clear terms.

Lastly, social morphology being clearly isolated from physiology, and the material base of the society being clearly distinguished from the physiological and psychological development of that society, one can perceive the solution of the difficult problem of relations between the material structure of societies on the one hand and the acts and representations of these societies, on the other. The facts which Durkheim discovered, but which he had so much difficulty in demonstrating in his *Division of Labour* to philosophers who did not believe in them and to economists who in their excessively narrow way reserved such study for themselves, are perfectly obvious to his successors and will be so for the next generation of sociologists. The number and density of population, the intensity of communication, and the relations between and divisions of age, sex, etc., state of public health, etc., appeared, as they are in fact, in direct relationship with all the phenomena of social activity. From there, through the mediation of activities, one can see emerging from the group itself, in its very structure, the great processes of sentiments, passions, desires; the great systems of symbolisms, images, ideas and prejudices; the great choices and the large-scale volitions of collectivities. Redescending the scale, one can see how humans come to group themselves around ideas, feelings, traditions and constitutions. One can also travel the path in reverse. From the special to the general, from the material to the ideal, the chains of analysis and synthesis thus become visible as continuous.

III. Simultaneous Use of the Two Methods of Division

The special divisions do not suffer from the imposition of this new division upon the accustomed one. On the contrary, thanks to this systematic study which makes them more flexible, they emerge enriched and clarified and, most important, legitimated. They find themselves back in place but renewed, being better ordered and better distributed; they recover their identity but no longer derive from prejudice. In fact, at this level, the important questions about the relationships of dependence and independence of the different social phenomena come to the forefront. They are easily decided, whereas up to this point, having been approached one by one by the different specialties, they have been encumbered with jargon and prejudices. For these questions threaten the specialities with serious pitfalls.

Nothing is simpler than the definition of the social phenomenon and nothing is more difficult than the definition of the various categories of social phenomena. The distinction is often very useful and relates merely to differences in viewpoints on the same thing. Thus moral theology can only with difficulty be separated from the rest of morality; etiquette from ritual, and vice versa. As for rules of appropriation, are they the expression of the economy or are they its foundation? This is matter for discussion. Depending on the angle of vision, an industry is an economic phenomenon or a technical phenomenon; indeed, it can be something altogether different: the cuisine in a good restaurant is also an aesthetic phenomenon. A holistic view can clarify these problems and facilitate these divisions. It also brings an awareness of their relativities. For there can be, and no doubt are, important phenomena in society which we still cannot assign to their true location. We scarcely know how to reserve the place that we keep for them.

This systematic study of relations permits us not only to situate but to 'deduce' the classical divisions of social physiology. In this connection it is necessary to use the procedure which A. Meillet has employed in this journal ('Comment les mots changent de sens', *Année sociologique*, IX, 1–38 (1906)) on the subject of the meaning of words: to see the various groups which are inspired with a single notion, and simultaneously or successively perform acts with different meanings, while they use a single word. The notion of efficacy is common to many parts of sociology, particularly in technology and in religion. Nevertheless, one sees their different points of application, even if a common origin is admitted. The Greeks contrasted law with nature, *nomos* with *physis*, in law, religion, art and aesthetics. The notion of rule is applied by the science of mores and by economic science. Nevertheless, one understands the important difference in these two fashions of conceiving the same thing, the same social attitude. Property is wealth, and vice versa; nevertheless, one conceives the relation of the two terms. Few subjects are more fascinating than these. Normally the greatest advances occur on the borders between the divisions of sociology, as on the borders between all sciences and parts of sciences, because at those points one sees the articulations of the facts and gets the best sense of the contrasts in points of view.

Naturally there are other sorts of progress, notably those on which Durkheim and his collaborators appear to have concentrated. They consist in deepening each of the various social sciences which sociology brings together. In our view, however, even these advances lead beyond the limits, so vast and yet still narrow, of law, the economy, religion, etc. They even consist often in a simple view of the complex historical reasons underlying a simple fact. Beneath the cold indifference of institutions, or beneath the fluctuation of ideas, every profound research exposes the living or conscious whole being, the group of humans. A constant going-and-coming, passing from the whole of society to its parts (secondary groups), to the instants of its life, to the types of action and representation; a special study of the movement of parts, joined however to a global study of the movement of the whole – this is how progress should be made not only in general sociology, but also in the special sociologies as well. Or rather, just as there is only one physics, perhaps indeed only one physical or physico-chemical phenomenon appreciated in different ways, so, even more evidently, there is only one sociology, because there is only one sociological phenomenon: social life which is the object of a single science, which approaches it from different points of view. And these points of view themselves are basically fixed by the historical state of civilisations, of societies, or their subgroups, of which our science is itself the product, and from the observation of which it set off. For example, it is not at all certain that if our civilisations had not already distinguished religion from morality, we would ourselves have been able to separate them. Thus these concrete divisions, which seem opposed to the special sociologies, actually supply methods for deepening them.

In particular it is an excellent way of explaining the different points of view from which humanity has considered itself and has made itself, and to which the special sociologies correspond. The latter exist only because the principal activities and their corresponding ideations have split up in the course of the extremely lengthy evolution of humanity over hundreds of millennia. However, if they have split up, it is because in relation to them, at least in a momentary fashion, the members of these societies have themselves split up. We are not always artisans or always religious, but when we are, it is generally in a workshop or in a church. In many cases, social activities have ended by dividing societies into numerous varied groups, more or less fixed. The study of these groupings or subgroups is, if not the purpose of sociological demonstration, at least one of its surest guides. To comprehend different social physiologies nothing is so useful as comprehending the different social structures to which they correspond.

There is no society known, or supposedly known, however primitive it may be, where there is not at least some classification of individuals. It was an error of genius on the part of Morgan to have thought that he had discovered the phenomenon of the horde of consanguine relatives; and it is only a hypothesis of Durkheim but, in our view, a necessary hypothesis, to postulate amorphous societies at the origin of all our societies. The difference between the sexes and generations and, very early on, exogamy, divided up societies. However, as soon as one enters history or ethnography, and no doubt from very ancient prehistoric times, societies are found to be divided in yet another fashion: into exogamous moieties, or more precisely into two primary exogamous clans or phratries, and into clans within these phratries, and into families. On the other hand, one already sees appearing here and there the nuclei of what will one day become the religious corporation and of what is already the magical corporation; one sees varieties of civil chieftainship, workshops with their technicians, bards – we allude here only to what has been ascertained in Australian societies, the most primitive of those that we know, but infinitely less simple than they are habitually represented as being. We may therefore offer the following rule: in a society, every social activity which has created for itself a structure and to which a group of humans is specially devoted, surely corresponds to a necessity in the life of that society. A society would not confer life and existence on that 'moral entity' or, as they say in English law, on that 'corporation', if the group (temporary though it may be) does not respond to the society's hopes and needs.

There is no absolute compulsion that these structures be permanent; they may last only for a time, and reappear later, often following a rhythm.

Particularly in the societies which have preceded ours or which still surround them (I mean all of those which do not belong to Asia, Europe and the Hamitic branch of North Africa), humans can organise themselves thus, without splitting permanently into functionally different groups. For example, in a number of ancient, or even contemporary, societies, at certain moments in public life, the citizens are divided into age classes, religious fraternities, secret societies, military troops and political hierarchies. All these organisations are different from the phratries, clans and families which nevertheless continue to subsist. They frequently become confused with these latter and with each other. These are the groups which in sum are charged with some specific function, or rather, this function *is* the life of the group. And the group is sustained, authorised, and endowed with a basic authority, by the entire society. The society abdicates in its favour, it delegates to it its force with respect to some ascertained goal. Thus, in the Negrito societies properly called, as in many of the Melanesian societies, justice is frequently the task of secret societies.

The study of these occasional, permanent or temporary groupings is necessary, beyond the exclusive study of representations and acts, for the mutual understanding of them all. The functioning of these groupings discloses which group is thinking and acting, and how it is doing so; this functioning reveals why the society relies on a group for this thinking and this action, why it opens itself to the group's suggestions, why it gives it a mandate to act. The analysis is completed when one has discovered who thinks and who acts and what impression this thought and action have on the society as a whole. From this point of view, even when in pretty rare cases the entire society feels and reacts, one can almost say that, in these moments, it acts as though it formed a special group. This becomes evident on exceptional occasions, when for some days or weeks the society congregates in its entirety, e.g., in certain Australian and American societies.

There is thus a kind of geometrical locus linking physiological and morphological phenomena: it is the secondary group, the special social structure which remains relatively isolated. There is a sort of mixed morphology. It assists in determining these secondary groups, i.e. the various organs of social life, whose separation lets us separate the various special sociologies, the latter (except for pure morphology) being basically all parts of social physiology. The latter thus comprehends, no less than does social morphology, the study of certain structures. Indeed, it is by describing these structures, by seeing how humans comport themselves in the church, at the market, in the theatre, and in the law courts that the special sociologies are best developed. What we propose is that, for all the different social structures and their activities, there be done what until now has only been done in depth for the clan and the family. This study of secondary groups, of the milieux which compose the total milieu which is society, the study of their variations, alterations and mutual actions and reactions is, in our opinion, not only one of the most desirable things, but the easiest and the most urgent of all. It is there, even more than in social practice – the institution being always in some degree congealed – that one finds the true life, material and moral at the same time, the behaviour of the group. Even the collective processes of ideation and representations can be treated in this fashion. It will seem very down to earth and indeed quite remote and inadequate to anyone who loves the vague and the ideal. In our opinion, it is the seekers for the ineffable who are mistaken. Contrary to what these seekers say, one is certain that there is a myth or a legend, that there is thought which is firm and deeply anchored, when there is a pilgrimage of saints, a festival, and clans or confraternities attached to these holy places. The play of collective ideas is serious when it is reflected in these places and in these objects, because it is taking place in the groups which, moreover, are endlessly created, dissolved and recreated by this game.

Thus this division of social phenomena into morphological and physiological and the division of the physiological phenomena into representations and collective acts may usefully be applied within the different special sociologies. Perhaps, indeed, it is truly essential to use this classification when studying separately social phenomena partitioned into religious, legal, economic, etc. The specialities segment the great classes of phenomena, so to speak, into vertically arranged heaps; however, these heaps can also be divided as it were into horizontal slices, by degrees or by increasing and decreasing levels of ideation, of greater or lesser materialisation depending upon whether one departs from or approaches the pure representation or the material structure properly so called. In our opinion, this division furnishes a methodological principle for the study of each major group of facts. It constitutes a sort of arithmetic proof that the analysis has been exhaustive. For a social phenomenon is explained in our view when one has discovered to what group it corresponds, *and* to what fact of thought *and* action it corresponds; whether it be physiological or morphological is of little significance.

The application of the principle is straightforward when it is a question of pure physiology. However, few sociologists employ it consistently, even though it is almost infallible in use. It forces one to see or to seek the acts beneath the representations, and the representations beneath the acts and the groups underlying both. Some series of institutions which on the surface appear to be composed exclusively of traditional practices or acts of manufacture, i.e. to be simply custom and techniques, are in fact full of notions which legal science and technology should disentangle. Other series of social facts which appear as purely rational, ideal, speculative, imaginative, or emotional and ineffable, like music or poetry, and science, are full of acts, activities, actions, of impressions on the senses, breathing, and muscles, or of practices and techniques.

Conversely, social morphology which serves as a control for the physiology, should also be subjected to these analyses. The group will thereafter never appear inert or unconscious. It is explained by its unity, and by its desire to live in common and its habit of doing so. These factors, over and above the gathering of the whole society, are made up of all these multitudes of imponderables, tendencies, instincts, imitations, communicated ideas, transient emotions, not to mention common inheritance.

This justifies the profound idea of German metaphysics, philosophy, and even thought in general, indeed of the multitude in Germany, namely the idea that a *Weltanschauung*, a 'conception of the world', governs action and even love. It is right to say that no less than a territory and a demographic mass, a tonality of life is what forms every society. Society in fact inspires a mental attitude, even a physical attitude, in its members and this attitude forms part of their nature. And these attitudes of these masses can be quantified – the first step in collective ethology.

Moreover, as we have seen, social morphology envisages society not only in space and numbers, but also in time. It studies movements, alterations and dynamisms. In addition, just as social psychology, or rather social physiology, expresses itself in the human material and, on occasion, in the social space and time where everything occurs, similarly the material structure of the group is never something indifferent to the consciousness of the group. The facts of morphology are frequently vital for it. For example, take the case of frontiers. One might think of them as entirely morphological and geographical; but are they not at the same time a moral and military phenomenon, and for certain peoples, particularly the ancients, a religious phenomenon?

The principal interest of these observations is that they permit us to expound, to systematise, and to demand the use of quantitative methods. To refer to material and social structures and the movements of these structures is to refer to things which can be measured. The link between the morphological and physiological allows one to estimate the considerable place which should be occupied by statistical research in all studies of social physiology. Subgroups and their actions can in fact be enumerated. One can take a census of occupations. Even crimes correspond, so to speak, to the subgroup of criminals.

Alas! Even in the *Année sociologique*, we are far from what is desirable. Statistics – social mathematics – even though it is itself sociological in origin, seems for us to be reduced to the usual problems of population (morphology); criminology and civil status (moral statistics); and the economy, that part of our sciences which boasts of being the domain of number and of the laws of number, as indeed it is in part. This limitation in the use of statistics is wrong. Basically, every social problem is a statistical problem. The frequency of the fact, the number of participating individuals, the repetition through time, the absolute and the relative importance of the acts and their effects in relation to the rest of life, etc. – all this is measurable and should be counted. The attendance at the theatre or at sports events, or the number of editions of a book, tell us far more about the value attached to a work or to a sport than do pages and pages by moralists or critics. The strength of a church is measured by the number and the wealth of its temples, by the number of its believers and the magnitude of their sacrifices and, though it is always necessary to consider also the imponderables in them, to consider only faith and theology is a no less serious error than to forget them. Managed with prudence and intelligence, statistical procedure is not only the means of measuring but the means of analyzing every social fact, because it forces us to perceive the acting group. It is true that many contemporary statistical studies themselves are rather inspired by the administrative or political needs of states, or indeed are poorly funded or badly directed by functionaries deficient in enlightened curiosity; they present a jumble. The true studies are still to be undertaken. However, we already know how far the historian and the sociologist of the coming generations will be better armed than we were. Already in our day, in immense works, like those of the American Census or the Census of India, one can watch the appearance, through the compiled statistics, of social things coming to the boil: the 'sorcerer's cauldron' where a society is fashioning itself. In the studies thus undertaken, the framework of all the special divisions itself is enriched.

IV. Utility of this Division for a Concrete General Sociology

This division has its advantages particularly from the viewpoint of general sociology. It prepares for the latter directly. In this concrete sociology, a better and better description has been given of the relations which exist between the different orders of social facts considered all together and considered separately: morphological and physiological on one side, and, at the same time, religious, economic, legal, linguistic, etc. One can now truly undertake the establishment of a sociology that is simultaneously general yet concrete.

The method is simple: study all the relationships. On one side, indeed, general sociology consists in the discovery of these relations.

This name of general sociology, however, invites error. It is not the pure domain of pure generalisations, certainly not of hasty generalisations. Above all, it is the study of general phenomena. We label as 'general' those social phenomena which extend to the whole of social life. But they may be entirely particular and precise; they can be lacking here and there, and even be limited to particular societies. These general phenomena are those of tradition, education, authority, imitation, social relations in general, between classes, the state, war, the collective mentality, reason, etc. We neglect these great phenomena and probably will neglect them for a long time to come. But others do not forget them. Regarding authority, the book by Professor Laski may be cited. Durkheim and the supporters of *Social Pedagogics* discuss education. Other authors reduce even sociology in its entirety to the considerations of general facts: this is the position of Simmel and his students, and that of Professor von

Wiese and his *Beziehungslehre*. We are not much in accord with them, but they are right in refusing to consider the study of these social building blocks as relevant only to legal sociology. We shall return endlessly to the state and the necessity for its study in connection with *applied sociology* and *politics*.

Another part of general sociology concerns the relations of social facts with neighbouring facts. Now, from this latter point of view, the relations of sociology with the two directly neighbouring social sciences, biology and psychology, become visible. The connections between social morphology, the science of the human material, and biology are clear. Those between social physiology and biology are less so. But if one grasps the fact that the morphological phenomena are the middle terms, the raisons d'être which link social ideas and actions to biological facts and vice versa, and the latter to ideas, etc., everything is clarified. A population has an ideal of beauty and creates a physical type by the action of this ideal on marriage and the birth rate. A population has a certain number of insane persons; these insane commit suicide or perpetrate crimes following the seasons and the number of hours of daylight, i.e., following the action of nature on the length and the intensity of social life. We mention only well-known facts.

The relation between psychology and sociology is also clarified in this way. The psychology of representations, and that of acts and that of characters come to correlate no longer with all sociological phenomena, but with those of the corresponding social phenomena: collective representations and acts, characterology, etc. And the problems of borders, important as they are, where psychology and the individual adjoin sociology and the social, are posed in terms of facts – facts of language, religious and moral sentiments, etc.

Finally, we shall mention three of the parts of general sociology which, in our opinion, could benefit immediately from a method of this kind. These are the theory of symbolism; the theory of reason; and finally the theory of collective characteristics. The first two are stated at present with extreme generality. (See the previous volume of the *Année* and in this volume the analyses of the works by Cassirer.) The last was very much in vogue in the time of Taine. Today it is out of fashion – wrongly, in our opinion.

The problem of thought, at once practical and theoretical, that of its relation with language, symbol and myth, and that of the relation between science and technology find here their normal and precise place, because they may all be considered together.

1. *The problem of language and symbol* (and the more general and more crucial problem of expression) is at once released from the speciality within which it has been shut by the linguists and the students of aesthetics, and from the generalities with which philosophers and some psychologists operate. These two essential things, so intimately linked, namely knowledge and symbols of all orders, appear finally as they are: linked to the totality of the group's activities and to the very structure of the group, and not simply to one or another

category of these activities. For there exist symbols and knowledge in economics, as in religion or law, and not simply in mythology and art. And the totem or the flag symbolise the group.

2. More generally, studies of 'mentality', of the 'making of the human mind', of 'construction and edification' of *reason*, are once again fashionable. These are what Comte had in view. Durkheim, Hubert, the writer, and others, among them Lévy-Bruhl and James Harvey Robinson, have restored them to honour in precise terms, we believe. They can and should be enlarged. Basically, they assume simultaneous knowledge of numerous elements in numerous civilisations. The data which must be taken into account are aesthetic, technical, and linguistic, and not only religious or scientific. Here too, mixtures must be detected and quantitative proportions must be established. After this has been done, it is necessary to stir up the mixture and to synthesise it in terms still more precise. This will bring to light the factor of 'totality' in history: the empirical, the illogical, and the logic of the beginning, the reasonable and the positive of the future. So long as numbers had a mystical and linguistic value, in addition to their technical and intellectual use; so long as illnesses were something moral or religious – for instance, sanctions for sin, arithmetic and medicine possessed a different orientation from the one they have now taken. Nevertheless they existed. The first pages in Hippocrates admirably mark the internal revolution which one day in Ionia turned medicine into a science. Our arithmetic itself continued to develop by the study of magic squares and mystical roots long after Pythagoras, right down to the seventeenth century. Our pharmacopoeia of the seventeenth and even of the eighteenth century came from civilisations which blended all kinds of strange observations in their pathology and their therapy, but who had some very solid knowledge of pharmacy – Arabia, India, China. Among the pharmacists, as among the alchemists, there was more than faith and empiricism: there was science. Reason and intelligent experiment are as old as societies and perhaps more durable than mystical thought. Thus again by viewing the whole pattern, one prepares the analysis of collective consciousness.

3. Studies of *mentality* are basically only one part of studies of *civilisation* and of *ethology*, which we discriminate very badly. Someday it will be necessary to separate them. For the moment, *collective ethology*, so difficult to establish, as we have seen, may consider them together. These analyses of the soul of a society or a civilisation may be compared to chemical analyses. According to Durkheim's profound views, just as in the case of individual characters, the characters of societies and civilisations are simply composites of measurable elements.

Types of social life which are more or less widespread are what we term *civilisations*. In one or another society, the principal characteristics of social life are more or less autochthonous, coming in greater or lesser part from more or less adjacent societies. Societies are more or less closed. For example, the Christian Middle Ages were a universe, a 'universitas', a catholicity, to a much greater degree than is contemporary Europe, and yet the groups which formed it were infinitely more diverse and more numerous. They were, however, less organic, and this is why they were infinitely more permeable to each other, weaker vis-à-vis influences from above; they still bore the imprint of the Roman Empire. Consequently, the higher levels of the still poorly-defined nations, the Church, the university, the principal corporations, the great brotherhoods, including chivalry, were much more internationalised than is true today. So much for the notion of civilisation.

As for the character of the members of a society, it singularises the society. Certain societies are more devoted to the search for the ideal and the aesthetic, or to commerce. Others are more devoted to the practical arts, to administration and government; this is the classic contrast of Greece and Rome. The lamented Paul Huvelin returned brilliantly to this subject *apropos* Roman law. Dr Jung and Mr Seligmann go so far as to speak of the psychoanalysis of races and societies, and even speak of 'introversion' and 'extroversion' with reference to them. They push Freudianism or Jungianism a little too far. These classifications do not have too much value in psychology and individual physiology; they have scarcely more in sociology. They do, however, impart some sense of the nature of a science of social orientations and, if such a thing exists, of racial orientations.

In fact, societies can be classified from multiple points of view. Thus, some are dominated by the youthful element, e.g., Russia, others by aged masses, e.g., France. From another point of view, they may be mostly rural (Russian) or mostly urban (English), agrarian or industrial, etc. Here one can take up again – in other terms than Steinmetz, but still pursuing the same goals as he did, ('Classification des types sociaux et catalogue des peuples', *Année sociologique*, III, 43–147 (1900)) – the vast question of the classification of societies, or rather of a catalogue of them. For basically Steinmetz was concerned with quantitative proportions, in a manner that was remarkable for his era.

Pursued in detail, these classifications will perhaps someday succeed in explaining the specificity of each known society, in explaining its special type, its individual aspect. At bottom this is what is done unwittingly, but not without method, by the historians, the practitioners of 'history' that has finally become 'social'. Perhaps we shall even succeed in explaining the idiosyncrasies and finally in diagnosing separately the precise state of each at every moment. All of these problems will escape from generalities and from political or even historical literature. Thus in the same way that psychology should be crowned by a 'characterology', so a 'characterology of societies', and a concrete 'collective ethology' will round out general sociology and will assist in understanding the actual behaviour of each society.

At that time, we may be able to do what we cannot now do without danger for the societies themselves, namely to raise the problem of *applied sociology* or *politics*. We will be ready to take this dangerous step and cross the gap which extends from pure social science in the direction of action.

However, as will be noted, these two plans for a pure sociology include nothing which concerns politics. On this point, we encounter contrary traditions from respectable sociologists. We must explain our position on this other discipline, politics, of which we are not practitioners.

Chapter 4

The Place of Applied Sociology
or Politics

One of the principal advantages of a complete and concrete knowledge of societies, of the types of societies, of each society separately, and of ours in particular, is that it permits us finally to glimpse what *applied sociology* or *political sociology* could be. The latter must be relentlessly eliminated from pure sociology. Nevertheless, – the only thing we can do here – one does glimpse quite separately some principles for the application of our sciences.

Politics is not a part of *sociology*. The two kinds of research are still excessively mingled even today. We insist on their separation. This is contrary to the American tradition, which has clearly been 'meliorist' since Lester Ward. American sociologists generally have the vivid sentiment that 'civics', 'politics', 'social service', 'social work' – in general 'social forces' and 'ethics' – are also theirs and constitute their domain. They confuse them with sociology. In contrast, we here in France and in the *Année sociologique* deliberately do not concern ourselves with politics. For that we have a reason of principle which Durkheim often pointed out and made precise: those who create this confusion between science and art are making a mistake both from the viewpoint of science and from that of art. The search for applications should be neither the object nor the goal of a science; it would be to falsify science. And art does not have to wait for science – the latter has no such primacy.

However, if sociology must remain pure, it must be concerned with its application. Durkheim said that it would not be worth 'an hour's trouble' if it had no practical utility. Like all speculation, it must in fact correspond to a technique. Furthermore, Durkheim knew that positivist politics and sociology have the same origin and were born of the great movement which rationalised social action at the beginning of the nineteenth century. (See his *History of Socialism*, which we are preparing for publication.) Thus in thinking about the application of sociology, we remain faithful to tradition. The only reproach which can be made against Comte, the first student of Comte, and against Spencer, the reason why they went astray, is that they thought they could legislate on the basis of extremely general reflections and very summary researches, although they could verify neither of these. The classical economists avoided generalities, but not these normative pretentions. It is true that they are more advanced than most of the other zealots of the political sciences. However, they are hardly better positioned to direct practice; except on certain points of financial legislation and banking practice, real life scoffs heartily at their predictions.

Science, then, should be applied, but its applications should not be confused with the science itself. The reasons for the current confusion are instructive. Let us repeat what Durkheim has said on this subject, in slightly different terms.

If this error has been committed by so many learned writers, it is because sociology is closer than any other science is to its corresponding practical art, namely politics, at least to the politics of modern times. Both assume that, apart from all religious, moral or other prejudices, society is aware of itself and of its evolution on the one hand, and of its milieu on the other hand, and uses this awareness to regulate its action. All the other practices and industries have an external and extra-conscious material object which imposes upon them attitudes which one knows beforehand may meet with only limited success; even pedagogy and psychiatry have a different object from psychology, particularly introspective psychology – namely the humans who are to be observed, and then either healed or taught. In contrast, politics and sociology have only one and the same object: societies. People imagine that they know everything about these latter, because they appear to their members as simply being composed of themselves, of their wills, and their ideas which are malleable at will. They believe their art to be sovereign and their knowledge to be perfect.

Precisely because the art, i.e., rational and positive political practice, is so close to the science of societies, the distinction between the two is more necessary than anywhere else. It is not enough to prettify actions with the aid of statistics which were themselves prepared on preconceived or manipulated plans following the ideas of the parties and of the moment, in order to impart to this action the appearance of being non-partisan, serene, social, free of all impure mixture and of all bias. Neither is it enough to be a sociologist, even a competent one, to lay down laws. Practice, too, has its privileges. Frequently, indeed, the defectiveness of science is such that it is better to trust to nature, to the blind and unconscious choices of the collectivity. It is frequently much more rational to say that 'no one knows' and to permit the natural imponderables to seesaw back and forth – those matters of consciousness of which one does not know to what precisely they correspond, namely interests and prejudices. The latter clash with one another in the courts, the press, the exchanges, and legislatures; they find expression in the *ethos* and the *pathos* of orators, in legal maxims, the proclamations of momentary leaders, the sovereign orders from capitalism and religion, campaigns in the press, elections with their verdicts clear and unclear. And it is better to let these forces act. Conscious ignorance is better than lack of awareness. The confession of impotence dishonours neither the doctor, the statesman, nor the physiologist, any more than it dishonours the sociologist. This 'complex' – so rich in conscious minds, bodies, times, things, ancient forces and latent forces, chances and risks which is a society – should usually be treated as an immense unknown by the humans who claim to direct it – whereas they are directed by it, or at most they attempt to express its movement by the symbols furnished them by language, law, contemporary morality, bank accounts, currencies, etc.

This is not said in order to diminish, but on the contrary to exalt the political art and its originality. The politician's turn of mind, his skill in wielding formulas, at 'finding the rhythms' and the necessary harmonies or unanimities, and in sensing contrary views are similar in kind to the artisan's dexterity: his talent is equally precious, equally native or traditional, equally empirical and equally effective. Science is only rarely creative. The lawyer, the banker, the industrialist, the religious leader, are all entitled to act by virtue of their practical knowledge and their talents. It suffices to have administered or commanded to know that the activity demands a practical tradition, and that it also demands something that a mystical psychologist would translate in terms of the ineffable, namely gift. Thus reason either theoretical or practical can justify a despotism by science. When this distinction between art and science, and this recognition of the primacy (at present) of the political art have been well established, only then can sociology intervene and thereby justify its material existence, i.e., the social function of sociologists.

I. The Sociology of Politics: A Part of General Sociology

First of all, it is possible to construct the science of this art. And this science of political notions concerns us. Not what in certain quarters are termed the moral and political sciences – the science of finance, diplomatic science, etc. Most frequently these so-called sciences are simply vulgar mnemonics, compilations of official circulars and statutes, less well digested than the old codes. They are merely catalogues of precepts and actions, handbooks of formulae, anthologies of maxims of social technique. Indispensable, of course, they clutter the streets with their pretensions and the schools with their professorships; the teachings they offer are merely apprenticeships, pure and simple. Nevertheless, sometimes, here and there, some profit can be derived from their works. Some powerful minds have raised their theorising to the level of articulating the principles of these arts, to clarifying this genre of social activity and social thinking, which presides over the very functioning of custom and law. At the present day in France, jurists such as M. Hauriou and L. Duguit are engaged in considerable effort to articulate the principles of public law. In Germany, the jurist-moralists, R. Wilbrandt and G. Radbruch and others, have had such an impact on their regions that they have attained political positions. A certain number of the best theorists of politics in America, in the first rank Prof. Merriam, have come to sociology under their own steam, starting from practice itself. We shall review the work of the latter. Elsewhere, an awareness of the task has been the act of the civilisation or society itself. The prestige of Roman law, of Greek politics and morality, of 'Hindu wisdom', of Jewish idealism, stem from the clarity of mind of these peoples. With force and precision they articulated their visions, the central symbol among the other symbols of their action. The English also have had their *prudentes* [sic], those of the common law, as well as of politics and constitutional law. A long series of writers from Hobbes to Austin must be ranged among the true founders of politics and sociology. An English lawyer knows naturally, so to speak, what is the meaning of sovereign. One should not underestimate the benefits of such bursts of human genius. The lucky discovery and research of these achievements of collective consciousness form the best foundation for present-day studies of sociology and politics. For once, the Historical School with its pure observation rightly dominates; still, it draws its starting point and the substance of its ideas from the implicit theories as well as from the explicit theories of all periods.

Except, it is still too backward; it considers only forms and constitutions. At this point sociology can give it an important stimulus. Normally, even in a parliamentary or a rule-governed regime, even in our own political arts which claim to be positive and empirical, which attempt to base themselves on statistics and numbers, even in our business dealings, where the accountant's art renders so many good services, – even in these contexts, it is the unconscious and the need evoking its satisfaction, it is action that dominates. The action is enlightened, certainly, neither blind nor mystical, yet it remains either unanalysable or only slightly analysed. Still it *is* possible to fashion a theory of the political art, first with the aid of those moments of consciousness of the collectivity itself, which knows how to choose and inspire its governors; then, with all the methods of comparative history, which permit analysis of the facts; in a word, with the aid of a 'pragmatics', as Aristotle called it. One can constitute a science of the social art. This science is beginning to establish itself; it consists simply in perceiving, thanks to these data, already known in part, how and through what political methods men act, have known how to act or believed they were acting upon one another, and have used such knowledge and belief to divide themselves into varying social milieux and groups, and to affect other societies or the physical environment. One can see how the theory of that art forms part of a sociology which is simultaneously general yet concrete.

We locate this science of the social art in the *Année* among the disciplines relating to *moral and legal sociology* or in *general sociology*. We have already acknowledged these waverings. In the first case, we operate on the excuse that the phenomenon of the state is a legal phenomenon. This is true: the state, the political organ of the society, like the constitution and the establishment of a sovereign power, are legal and moral facts. Surely, however, they are much more. They converge on the totality of society, and everything in society converges towards them. How far? We cannot state this precisely, we can only help the reader to sense it. For example, the frontiers of the state, that hypersensitive point of society and the political state, are of a morphological order, as we have already said; and so on in that manner. The political art and the science of that art should, then, like sociology itself, take into account all the social facts. Particularly in our modern societies, economic and morphological (demographic) phenomena come within its jurisdiction. Quite particularly, some important matters that escape our headings, vis. tradition, instruction, and education, are essential parts of the state. We must then break the narrow framework of the juristic theory of the state. Political theory must be extended to include the all-encompassing action of the state. It is necessary to go even further and include subgroups: not only to analyse the action of the centre but also that of all the secondary groups, voluntary or involuntary, permanent or temporary, of which a society is composed.

In principle, this theory of the social art enlarges politics. From this viewpoint, its action is a benefit. For if the confusion of the problem of the state and sovereignty with a legal problem was disastrous, it constitutes an error of fact and practical error. To proceed in the accustomed fashion leads to the worst dangers. The founders of the positivist science of societies, who were also founders of the positivist politics, Saint-Simon and Comte, in turn called attention to this fault. They had a certain hatred of the lawmaker, of lawyers, of administration, and a certain fetishism for the 'industrialist', the 'savant', the 'producer'. This attitude has become traditional in socialism and continued into Bolshevism. Let us avoid these excesses, for the art of acting, commanding, and manoeuvring legally will always be essential to the common life, even to the technical life. The fact remains that, partly by the force of things and largely through inertia, our Western parliamentary systems leave too much to lawyers and publicists the care for interests which surpass the limits of law and bureaucracy. It will thus be particularly necessary to break with the ancient tradition which has dominated politics from the Lagide and Roman chancelleries right down to the privy councils of kings. Modern societies know that many eminently social matters should not be left to bureaucrats, councillors and lawyers. Issues which involve and even put in question society itself, e.g., war and peace, should be decided otherwise than has previously been the case. The principal service that sociologists have so far rendered to politics, and will increasingly render, by a theory of politics itself, consists in helping people to see the degree to which political problems are social problems. Consequently, they will go seriously wrong if, in order not to lapse into the common error, they all remain in their ivory tower, if they completely abstain from taking part, if they leave politics to politician theorists and to bureaucrat theorists. The art of social life concerns them particularly, and to transmit a tradition, educate the younger generations, integrate them into a particular society, 'elevate' them and particularly to make them progress, all of this surpasses the limits of law and of everything which by general agreement is called the state. The science of that art, then, forms part of general sociology, or, in a sociology which is divided in a concrete fashion, forms an entirely special part of the sociology of action.

II. Sociology and Politics

Conceived in this fashion, this theory of the political art is an essential part of sociology and more specifically, in our proposed divisions, a part of general sociology, and in this latter, a part of the theory of general adjustments. However, this science of the social and political art remains theoretical. Like the rest of sociology, it has for its principal method historical comparison or statistical analysis, even though the facts being compared are modern facts. For this reason, it is interesting, instructive and informative. It is, however, only a small contribution to the real direction of contemporary societies. The art of directing a society – action, administration, command – are things altogether more vital and powerful than this indirect influence of the science of societies. This 'action at a distance' is a relatively small matter in relation to politics as such. How can we contribute effectively to the latter? This is the final problem of sociology.

From contact with sociology, political action is already singularly augmented. Under the inspiration of sociology, political action is understood in a broad sense as including not only the direction of the organs of sovereignty, but also the control of financial forces, industries, education, and material, moral and intellectual relations with other nations. In addition, clarified, enhanced and refined by sociology, political action can be infinitely better conducted than if it is left to grope blindly. Thus, the political art should not be independent of sociology, and the sociology cannot be disinterested in political action. What, however, should be their relations? What place should be given to them in a complete sociology? Here are a few pointers.

First, we must repeat the wish of Spencer, reiterated by Durkheim, that knowledge of sociology should be required for a person to qualify as an administrator and a legist. In fact, in numerous countries, sociology forms part of the educational curriculum of the future bureaucrat and of numerous institutes of advanced commercial or administrative studies. Furthermore, again in fact, sociology clearly acts upon politics in our days. The latter has adopted an experimental and scientific attitude which, more than is generally believed, comes from our studies.

However, what should be the converse relationship? While we see clearly what we should demand of the politician, and even of the citizen who owes it to himself to become enlightened, what do these two have to claim from us? First of all, our attention. That is to say, the public does not let us concern ourselves exclusively with what is easy, amusing, curious and bizarre, the past, without danger, because it concerns societies which are either dead or remote from our own. They want studies with conclusions relevant to the present day. To this request one might be tempted to respond that science is sovereign, that its freedom of thought – that of scholars – must be without limit. For one never knows precisely which fact is decisive, even from the practical viewpoint. Frequently, a fact in our civilisations has its explanation in strange corners of the past or the exotic. Perhaps it is registered at the moment in obscure statistics; it can be born in our days, in the unknown gestations of unknown forms of associations invented in unknown levels even of our own populations. This has been seen. Cooperation was born in this way; syndicalism has extremely deep popular origins; Christianity lived in the catacombs; some major scientific and philosophical traditions have made their way in obscurity. However, with the right of scientific freedom reserved, it is necessary to make some effort.

First of all, it is necessary to be on the watch for these new movements of societies, to bring them quickly to the knowledge of the scientific public, to sketch out the relevant theory. In order to do this, a better division of effort would be necessary, and we ourselves should turn more to contemporary matters. The sociological observation of the institutions of the future has an interest at once theoretical and practical.

This, however, is not enough. The people itself expects of us a less purist, a less disinterested attitude. Even while refusing to sacrifice to a search for the good one instant which will not be exclusively devoted to the search for the true, it is obviously necessary that sociologists fulfil their social duty. They must help in directing opinion and even the government. Naturally, if a sociologist wants to act as a politician, he should, so far as he can, separate his science from his actions. However, it is possible to produce works on subjects that are less burning and more general, yet that are oriented towards moral practice and politics. It was thus that Durkheim conceived his 'morality'. This is why without delaying we published in the series of the *Travaux* of the *Année sociologique*, his *Moral Education*, which is not lacking in political pages; it is why we shall also publish his *Civil Morals and Professional Responsibility*. In fact, there is an entire domain, midway between action and science, in the region of rational practice where the sociologist can and should adventure.

Furthermore, from time to time, by chance, we can be sure of our predictions and even transform them at once into precepts. Scholars in the fortunate experimental sciences, so peaceable and so proud of their methods and their independence, often can apply their science to industry or medicine. They do not fear the confusion of two orders of researches. They have no dread of being undervalued, nor do they have a sense of shame at appearing either useless or useful. Likewise, it is necessary to impose our science as such, but one need not feel afraid of being confused with a man of action, when one can, when one has not 'sought', as the Bible says, and when one speaks only in the name of science itself. After having advanced the latter, one should attempt to utilise it. Moreover, on a good number of points, some of us sociologists have had a clear practical vision. The two Webbs in England and Emmanuel Levy, beginning from their theories of syndicalism and contract, have done much to establish new forms of the Collective Contract. The conclusions of Durkheim's book on *Suicide*, those which concern the occupational group, should be taught everywhere. Regarding inheritance, the lecture by Durkheim (*Revue Philosophique*, 1920), which is the conclusion of long and brilliant researches on the family merits the status of 'classic'. Let us, then, not fear to contribute these ideas and these facts to the debate. Will our practical conclusions be rare and of little contemporary relevance? All the more reason to propagate them liberally and energetically.

The sociologist can be useful to politics in still another fashion. Without interfering with it, nor with politicians nor with government bureaux, he can assist these latter by impartial inquiries, by the simple scientific cording of facts, even of facts that he does not know personally or cannot attempt to theorise.

The principle that we declare here is not a pious dream; it is an accomplished fact. During a journey which the munificence of a great American scientific institution made possible for us, we have seen the importance and the scale of a research movement of this kind in the United States. Powerfully assisted by individuals, states, and cities, sociologists transform the information available to the lawmakers and administrators of cities and major institutions. First of all, in their bureaux, states and cities have their own departments of research. There is, however, more. In place of statistics and reports which answer only administrative needs, complete enquiries have been instituted, for example, concerning certain cities. These have been assigned to sociologists or to independent statisticians, or again have been undertaken by these individuals separately from any administration, on their own initiative. Such, for example, is the case of the Institute of Social Research at Chicago, where economists and demographers, like Professor Marshall or Professor Hill, and sociologists, like Professors Park and Burgess, collaborate with Professor Merriam. Elsewhere, in place of arid discussions of law, in place of the old criminal statistics, statistics of courts and prisons, not of morality, there have been established major detailed judicial enquiries on Cleveland. The one directed by Professor Pound at Harvard for the whole state of Massachusetts, with the assistance of students and professors alike at the Harvard Law School, subjects to a precise analysis *each* of the cases which have been presented before the courts; and, subsequently, the 'tabulation' of these cases discloses the precise state of jurisprudence, public morality and the trends in both. Lawmakers, lawyers, and sovereign public opinion are thus impartially informed about themselves. The institutes of economic research are also numerous in that country (they are beginning to prosper in Germany). In one state, North Carolina, the Department of Social Science at the University is charged with legislative inquiries preliminary to the drafting of laws. This movement is only at its beginning.

In any case, the sociologist is professionally qualified as well as and better than bureaucrats to observe even the phenomena which the bureaucrats administer, because functionaries do not naturally possess the necessary impartiality and the clear view of affairs; above all they represent tradition, when they are not serving their own interests or those of a class which they serve.

Apart from the foregoing, what else can we do? Very little. But this would already be something. Some amongst us would be able to study, practically and theoretically at the same time, the new and old ideas, the traditional usages and the revolutionary novelties of those societies which, in these troubled times, seek to give birth to their own future. If some younger peoples, excited by great enterprises, could do that, the political data of our time and of each society, as regards both facts and ideals, could be studied separately and without prejudices. Contemporary matters could then form the object of a kind of intellectual accountancy, of constant 'appreciation', as Comte said. The first phase of positivist politics is to know and tell societies in general and each society in particular what they are doing and where they are going. The second phase of morality and of politics properly so-called consists in telling them frankly whether they are doing well, practically and ideally, by continuing to go in such and such a direction. The day when, alongside the sociologists, some political theorists or some sociologists themselves, in love with the future, achieve this firmness in diagnosis and a degree of reliability in therapy, propaedeutics and especially in pedagogy, will be the day when the cause of sociology has won. The utility of sociology will impose itself; it will impress an experimental formation upon the moral mind and on political education; it will be justified in fact, as it is already in reason.

The principal goal will thus be attained on the day when, separated from it but inspired by it, a positive politics comes as the application of a complete and concrete sociology. Although it may not give practical solutions, it will at least give the direction for rational action. Sociological teaching, information and training will give to the coming generations of sociologists a sense of the delicate quality of political processes. Unwittingly employed at the moment, these procedures will be brought to the desirable degree of awareness when one or two generations of scholars have analyzed the mechanisms of living societies, those which interest us practically. Politicians and men of action will no longer limit themselves to instinctive choices. Without waiting for an excessively developed theory, they will be able consciously to balance interests and rights, the past and future. They will be able, all the time, to assess the internal milieu that is society and the secondary milieux formed by generations, sexes, and social subgroups. They will be able to weigh the forces represented by ideas and ideals, currents of thought and traditions. Finally, they will be able to avoid misconceptions about the external milieux in which the interests that they administer are immersed: the other societies which can counteract them; the earth whose reserves must be administered with a view to future generations. Without Utopias, but without confusion with science, we have here a programme of positive politics.

Perhaps this programme will be found pretty limited. These conclusions are possibly disappointing for the political activist, or even for the 'social worker', for the zealot dedicated to 'social service', for the writers on 'civics', who at the moment are attaching themselves generously and no doubt effectively to activists. However, once the movement has started, other effects may follow. Many problems whose solution is sought head-on are not well posed; others, though well posed, are badly handled. The role of education is not championed by anyone, and yet it is perhaps the most important of all. The role of parties is enormously exaggerated by the historians, by the press, and by public opinion; the preponderance of interests, above all those of the subgroups, economic in particular, is really too great at this point. In contrast, the role of values, especially those of the subgroups, such as the occupational group, is underestimated. We have just raised many problems, essential ones, which the sociologists are raising, but which are not yet even being asked by the public, the legislature, and the bureaux. On the contrary, these latter would like to impose upon us their own problems, less important though they are. It can happen that sociology satisfies neither the sovereign bodies nor the different sections of our societies.

Perhaps indeed, even though it is useful, it may satisfy no one. Sociology is simply the principal means for educating society. It is not the means for rendering humans happy. Even the social art and politics are incapable of this, although they pursue this illusory goal. Durkheim showed this clearly. The only effect of science and art is to render mankind stronger and more a master of itself. The works of reason can only give the instrument to groups and to the individuals who compose them. It is upon these that the task falls to use it for their good..., if they wish..., and if they can.

Sociology, then, offers no panacea? That is not a reason to stop its progress. Quite to the contrary, the aim is to render the discipline useful by multiplying works and students.

We have lingered over these questions of method, only because the problem is precisely to attempt and straight away, at a moment when our studies are popular, to give to workers who participate therein the plan which will permit them to make the best choice for their works.

Note

1. Note on the notion of structure. We apologise for continuing to use the word 'structure'. In fact it designates three distinct things; (1) social structures which are truly material – the distribution of the population on the surface of the earth, near sources of water, in towns and houses, along roads, etc; the distribution of a society across sexes, ages, etc.; then other things, still material, but already moral, which nevertheless merit the designation of 'structure' since they are manifest in a permanent fashion in definite localities: the locations of industries; isolated secondary groups, for example, in a composite society, e.g., the Negro, Chinese, Italian quarters in a major American city; (2) we also label as 'structures' those subgroups whose unity is predominantly moral, even though it is expressed in unique habitats, specific agglomerations which are more or less durable, e.g, the domestic group, and, by way of illustration, the great family; a group of parishioners; clans which are no longer constantly isolated from one another and whose members are not always grouped in wards or in localities; (3) finally, we label as social 'structure' something which is no longer in the least material, the constitution of the society itself and the constitution of the sub-groups, e.g., a sovereign power, a headship within the tribe, clan or family; the age classes, military organisation, etc., all of them phenomena that are almost purely physiological, indeed almost exclusively legal. We would have liked to eliminate this confusion between facts of morphology and facts of physiology in our own nomenclature. We have tried to reserve for the last group of facts, the purely moral assemblages, the name of *constitutions*. However, the word fails to emphasise that in these facts there is nevertheless something other than law. For example, the companies of a regiment, the archers or the slingsmen of a tribe, have a place in the line of battle. Nevertheless, we shall try to dissipate all ambiguity by using adjectives and saying: *social* structure or *material* structure.

Additional Bibliographical Note

This memoir is published without notes. It would not have been difficult to transform it into a bibliographical catalogue of sociological methodology. But for that purpose, the *Année* is sufficient. Nor did it seem to us necessary to sketch a history of the question, nor even to attempt a systematic critique of the principal and most recent outlines of sociology. It would have been necessary to cite and discuss all the recent manuals and innumerable articles. The *Année* has performed that task and will continue to do so. Finally, in our opinion, questions of methods do not tolerate a great display of erudition, and merit only a certain argumentational sobriety.

We simply ask the reader to refer to two articles by Brown and Myers on social anthropology and the relations of anthropology and sociology, and to two recent articles by Tönnies and Thurnwald, of which this note is a kind of review; in any case these articles come within the same year as the *Année*, and this note may be attached to the bibliographical section of this volume.

Brown, A.R. 'The Methods of Ethnology and Social Anthropology', *South African Journal of Science*, XX:124–47.

Myers, J.L. 'The Place of Man and his Environment in the Study of the Social Sciences', *Report of the British Association for the Advancement of Science* (1923), 1924.

Tönnies, F. 'Eintheilung der Soziologie', *Zeitschrift für die Gesamte Sozialwissenschaft*, 1925, LXXIX:1–15.

Thurnwald, R. 'Probleme der Völkerpsychologie und Soziologie', *Zeitschrift für Völkerpsychologie und Soziologie*, 1925, I:1–20.

Radcliffe Brown differs from us only on the name and title of our science. He understands social anthropology exactly as we understand sociology. However, he arbitrarily restricts it to the so-called 'primitive peoples'. This distinction between social anthropology and the sociology of modern peoples is full of dangers for the two parts of a single science.

With Mr. Myers we are also in nearly complete agreement, believing as we do that human sociology is only part of the science of man or anthropology. We are simply more ambitious than he is; the domain of our sciences is considerably broader than the one he describes.

The two articles by Thurnwald and Tönnies are much closer to our subject. For Tönnies, sociology is divided into general sociology and special sociology, or sociology properly so called. (A) *General sociology* includes two sections: *social biology* with its descriptive part; social anthropology; ethnography or demography or sociography; and a second section, *social psychology*. (B) Sociology properly so called includes first: I. A *pure sociology* with the divisions dear to the author: (1) *theory of fundamental concepts*: community and society (*Gemeinschaft* and *Gesellschaft*); (2) *theory of social bonds* or social essences (duties, etc.), unity, etc. (classes, nations, etc., clans, etc.,); (we pass over other refined divisions); (3) a *theory of social norms* (order, law, morality); (4) a *theory of social values* (economic, political ideal); (5) a *theory of the products of society* (economy, cities, constitutions). This sociology properly so called also includes: II. an *applied sociology*, and finally, III. an *empirical sociology* or sociography which in part repeats social biology.

We recognise here the learned and complicated divisions by a veteran of our studies. They form the vast framework of an immense course. They are a canvas of personal suggestions, elaborated in personal fashion. They are not a plan of work. In certain aspects, however, Tönnies has anticipated the divisions which we propose in Chapter 3. Finally, he still remains in agreement with Durkheim on a capital point: he firmly claims for sociology the totality of the social sciences. He allows to escape only a small number of those facts which we believe are included in the social domain, for example, language.

We pass over the fact that Thurnwald distinguishes sociology from social psychology (*Völkerpsychologie*). Basically, this social psychology comprehends pretty well what we here call the physiology of collective representation. On the other hand, he always couples it with sociology, here and in all of his writings (cf. his articles, 'Zum gegenwärtigen Stande der Völkerpsychologie', *Kölner Vierteljahresschrift für Soziologie*, 1924, IV:32–43; 'Zur Kritik der Gesellschafts-psychologie', *Archiv für Sozialwissenschaft*, 1924, LII:462–99). The total formed by social psychology and sociology thus represents everything that we simply call sociology. There is only a difference of words. In addition, the strictly sociological method of Thurnwald is exactly what Durkheim advocated: descriptive, comparative, explaining all social phenomena, including the role of the individual ('Probleme', p. 12), by other social phenomena. Moreover, this is how Thurnwald has proceeded in his numerous articles, often original and profound, which we here recommend, in the *Real-Lexicon der Vorgeschichte* by Max Ebert (1925–). The ensemble of these articles will constitute a kind of dictionary of sociology. The article, 'Probleme', which serves as the preface to the new review which he edits, is full of suggestions in this direction.

We have, nevertheless, to regret one thing. Thurnwald accepts, or seems to us to accept, a certain location of sociology within general sociology. He is midway between the American sociologists and us. Under this head, we address to him the same criticisms that we later address to our confrères. We are struck by his enumeration of problems, as well as by the organisation of them which he has made, for two years, in the critical section of his review. All are interesting. All are well posed, in terms which show his effort to escape from 'verbal symbols' (ibid., p. 19). The indefinite rights of sociology are clearly marked for each. Still we are unable to agree on the whole ensemble. Not all the problems are stated; for example, those of anthropogeography or the history of religions, or of linguistics or aesthetics are not named as such, and are only envisaged from extremely general points of view, more or less exclusively from the viewpoint of their psychological possibility. Indeed, we would even say that Thurnwald is willing to leave them entirely to the specialists, if we did not know that he proceeds otherwise in his own work. Nor are problems which surpass the limits of general sociology explicitly raised. A few examples of his headings: milieu and disposition; political forces; labour and economy; law and legislation; contemporary movements; contrasts between civilisations (*Eine Kultur im Spiegel der anderen*); variations and forms of thought. The divisions are obscure. In his 'Führerschaft und Siebung', (*Zeitschr. f. Völkerps. u. Soz.*, II, 1926, 1–19) Thurnwald has given an example of the way in which they should be handled. This heading is untranslatable into French or English. One can say equally well 'commandement et selection' (command and selection), or 'autorité et filtrage' (authority and filtering), 'direction et choix' (direction and choice); in English, 'leadership and selection' does not even convey the subject; but the subject is happily chosen and treated concretely, albeit summarily.

Next, the very order of the problems is incomprehensible to us. Why does 'Primitive thought' come after 'Personality'? We cannot grasp the rationale.

Finally, a last point of divergence is rather serious. Thurnwald assigns a considerable role to biological data (animal sociology) and particularly to psychological data (*Persönlichkeit*). In our opinion, these are not of direct concern to sociology. Intelligence, character, sex, abnormality, etc., are all of them what we call biological and psychological conditions of social facts. They should only be regarded as conditions; in our view they belong only to the special sciences; they are not part of our métier. Naturally, this does not mean to say that we should be unaware of them. Quite the contrary; we fully agree with Thurnwald on what we would call the psychological and biological effects of social life: the formation of races, etc., the effects of alcoholism, etc. All of this in fact should be studied by the sociologist, and can only be well studied by him. The present plan for 'Researches on Social Psychology and Sociology' (five volumes are announced), edited by Thurnwald, is equally characterised by this mixture of animal sociology, biology, pure or applied psychology (psychology of occupational activity), and politics, together with pure sociology.

Thurnwald has assembled numerous collaborators. But he restricts the work of his troops to problems which we too consider as important, but which are far from being the only problems. However, he appropriates to himself groups of scholars whose independence we respect. In general their method is the same as ours, but they group themselves differently. Our best wishes to him and to them.

In any case, all of the foregoing relates only to questions of the division of scientific labour. What matters is that the work be done, and be done well. The *name* of the science that will claim the credit is of minor significance.

Index